# JOSEPH FULTON

## SCARRED

### A MEMOIR of ADVERSITY and ANGELS

*Scarred: A Memoir of Adversity and Angels*
©Joseph Fulton

Print ISBN 979-8-35091-742-0
eBook ISBN 979-8-35091-743-7

*For the angels that saved a life*

# CONTENTS

# FOREWORD BY OWEN

I can't believe Joe asked me to write this foreword. Honestly, my wife just told me that it's not "forward," it's "foreword." Really? Joe's messing with me or gauging my writing skills just in case he needs a backup. Regardless, it's an honor for him to ask me out of all the people he could have chosen.

I met Joe, or Joef as we called him, back in college. He and his ex-girl-friend (thank God) were playing beer pong; a friend and I were distracting his shots. Joe's face was disgusted and totally flustered at the antics we were pulling. They ended up losing, and Joe was pissed at me. That was my very first encounter with him.

Somehow, we ended up reconnecting a year later. We had mutual friends, and he lived in a ten-person house with the rest of our group. I thought Joe would hate me forever. Luckily, I was wrong. After reliving the story, we laughed it off, and this was the moment I started to realize how cool Joe was. That's when I started learning a little more about him.

He was a pre-medicine major and worked his tail off, always reading, studying, and working a full-time job. But he was a fun guy—hitting up the bars, cliff jumping, staying up on roofs to soak in the night sky with friends, racing shopping carts down steep hills, coming home and showing me his black eye from a fight. He stood up for his friends. He stood up for himself. He was the good guy everyone wanted to be surrounded by.

After graduation, we made it a point to stay in touch and continue our friendship. It was pretty easy because I worked in the same city he lived in.

We coined the term "Man-Movie Monday," where he'd come over to the apartment to watch something. We spent time at our favorite pizza joint. Or he would sneak me into his pharmacy school library so I could study for my MBA. We often talked about making big moves and what our careers would be like. We decided on future millionaires and world leaders.

It's always good to have friends who push you to be a better version of yourself; Joe is that kind of friend. Instead of things like "yeah, that's going to be tough" or focusing on how difficult things might be, he'd say "go for it" or "why not you?" He's the kind of guy that gives you confidence in yourself. Seeing how hard he works always motivated me to do the same. We both made it through graduate school, and we had plans to take over the world.

I got married and started a family. I remember how excited my wife and I were to finally get the baby to bed, and I saw Joe calling.

I picked up the phone and heard a worrisome voice that I wasn't familiar with. He said, "I'm just going to say it. I have a brain tumor."

I was shocked.

*Are you sure?*

*How do you know?*

*What doctors have you seen?*

Those were the first things to run through my mind. Right as we were getting our journeys started. . . this wasn't part of the blueprint. I remember feeling stunned. How could someone his age end up with a brain tumor? I thought that was something you see more in the older population.

Oh, and he was prepping for brain surgery the next week, where they would need to cut open his skull and remove as much of the tumor as possible. . . um, what?

Watching Joe over the past five years with this battle has been brutal, inspirational, sad, and a total mix of emotions. I know life isn't fair, but c'mon, this really isn't fair.

He's worked too hard. He's come too far. He's landed his dream job. WE HAD A PLAN.

A brain tumor was not part of it. Joe has managed to battle through this, and it is a battle. Multiple surgeries, tons of medications, and the damn seizures. I usually don't hear him complain, so when I do, I try my best to listen.

Of all the things he has to go through, I hate the seizures most. It's really the only time I see him get down. My family prays for Joe every night that the seizures subside. The worst part about the seizures is the unknown. The unknown damage they're doing, the unknown medication or a combination of medications to alleviate them, and the unknown reason they're happening in the first place. . . and I hate that.

Joe has managed multiple relationships, dating, friendships, travel, jobs, holidays, and life through all this. He will continue fighting, and I hope he never lets it overcome his spirit and drive. As a friend, it's been hard to watch, but it really puts things into perspective. What really matters in life is to not sweat the little things and never take a healthy day for granted.

We went to the driving range to hit golf balls a few weeks back, and he showed me his phone with a book cover. When he told me he wrote a book a few months post-brain surgery, I was surprised, but then I wasn't.

"What a better way to recover and rehab than writing and reading," he said.

In typical "Joe fashion," he didn't just rehab casually; he did so productively and efficiently. He's done it before and will continue to inspire me, his family, his friends, and now anyone that reads this book.

Thank you for the opportunity to write this FOREWORD for your book.

# PREFACE

*"If you change the way you look at things, the things you look at change."*

—*Wayne Dyer*

This book was written for anyone who is struggling silently, doesn't really know who to reach out to, and has no idea where their life will take them. I will include myself in that category. We all have battles we don't really talk about and the ones we don't even want in the first place, but they knock on our doors anyway.

"Everyone has something going on" is a phrase I remind myself of daily. In the age of social media, people only prefer posting about the best of times that they have. If I talk about my life, it has transformed into many things that I can't do anymore due to my illness. It's not just those dumb panoramic videos from the top of a mountain or alcohol-induced pictures from a party. It could be the possibility of never having children, or the fear of getting married only to leave a widow behind, or the risk in solo travel overseas just in case anything happens to me. But I know social media is not a real-life depiction of what is going on behind the scenes.

The fact is nobody has a perfect life, no matter how great it may seem. Fights within the family, arguments with their spouses, stress over a job, death of loved ones, and maybe some of the same worries I'm experiencing. Thus, social media is not for the purpose of maintaining contact with people's lives anymore. Rather, it is feeling the pressure to show off, and it can generate physical and mental symptoms. Call me an old man who is not keeping up with the times. Maybe it's my diagnosis that made me wish for a time before these platforms emerged.

They're a façade. That is why I limit my use of social media, sometimes refraining for weeks, knowing that these fun posts don't cover the full story of a person. Only through one-to-one talks can I truly learn about what's going on in someone's life.

People are always going through something as bad or even worse than I am, especially as we age. My intention was to write this book, keeping that in mind. I even felt guilty at times, complaining about what I am going through. Others have their own story to tell, too. This is just mine. I have written stories about friends who are living in silence with their grief.

One of my goals was to list examples of other people who have directly affected me, those undergoing their own battles, and the adversity family and friends have overcome. This aspect is a constant reminder that things happen that are out of our own control.

But there must be a channel to release all of that stress.

Nobody should refuse help if they need it. I released my stress with my therapist, my doctors, and occasionally with friends and family. And sometimes, it's necessary to open the floodgates. I wanted to demonstrate the feelings I've had and list ways that I dealt with my problems. In some cases, I have handled things correctly. In others, I have certainly not.

I can see my life before and after my diagnosis with a brain tumor. I didn't recognize that man before all of this happened. This book allowed me to reflect on things in the past, some of which I had dismissed. I didn't know if I should hold on to those minor but specific details. Some examples undoubtedly brought a form of PTSD, which was sad but confusing to me. I struggled with its meaning. . . why would I have to endure this? Was this meant to happen? Was it a case of bad luck mixed with science? Did I need this to test if I could overcome it all?

This book became endless hours of therapy, all wrapped into one.

There is a need for me to feel a certain part of a connection to those who have suffered. Sometimes I feel lonely, often self-pity. And then I sit down, gazing at all the houses around my neighborhood. I suddenly come back down to earth. In the house to my right, a man has developed early-onset dementia. Across the street, a woman lost her husband earlier this year due to a slip-and-fall accident. To my left, spouses are going through a divorce with four little kids having to witness, one of whom is just a baby. Illness or not, I don't envy anyone on my block. Sadly, it's a part of life, and it comes with being human.

It is a grueling process to love yourself unconditionally and find acceptance in it. There is no other option but to do the best you can with the struggles you're given. That is my hope for everyone who reads this book.

Throughout my life, I've had to accept things day by day, year by year. Most of them have been good! My life is not a sob story in the least. Yes, there are difficulties and challenges that come with living. You have no choice but to make peace with them. I didn't handle my diagnosis of cancer like a hero in the beginning. I've learned to accept most things that have come around. Acceptance is an ongoing process.

The first time around is always the worst because you're still comprehending what it's like to have a chronic illness, but it's how you deal with those struggles that turn you into a fighter.

Grieve, get up again, and try your best. I've learned how to deal with things better. Otherwise, I would not have known without experiencing symptoms firsthand. I've learned what my seizures would be and how to accept them. My relationships, be they romantic or with friends, have changed. I know how to handle them and what my expectations should be. I have come to know what judgment and discrimination feel like. Physical pain, mental pain, emotional pain—I've been through it all. I don't fear

MRIs anymore, rather anticipating when the day comes that I'll be prepared when it changes for the worst.

Most of all, my faith has wavered through the years since I was diagnosed. Going from "Why me" to "Why not me" has become my greatest hurdle.

Do whatever you can: Use the resources available to you and find a sense of joy. I hope that you find a community that embraces you as I have. Use your power in this fight for good and not evil. Find your strengths. No matter what you are dealing with, you are not alone. Learn to deal with your ailment in some way that helps others; by doing so, you may find peace and love in your grief.

# CHAPTER 1:

# THE RUDE AWAKENING

*"His soul sat up. It met me. Those kinds of souls always do—the best ones. The ones who rise up and say, "I know who you are, and I am ready. Not that I want to go, of course, but I will come." Those souls are always light because more of them have been put out. More of them have already found their way to other places."*

My eyes rest on the words a little longer than they should, as many thoughts run into my head frantically. I shake my head a little in an attempt to clear my mind and read the glorious words written by Markus Zusak once again. The above-mentioned lines are narrated by the Death itself as it comes to collect the souls into its papery palms.

Before I move on to the next section, another thought chimes into my mind. It's more like a question I would like to share with my readers.

Do you think we are ready for death? I mean, if someone told you that your time is up, would you freak out, or would you think for a brief moment before nodding your head and shrugging, "Okay?"

Let me tell you something: The majority of us, if not all, are never ready for death. Why is that so? There are many reasons, but some of the most common ones may include: we do not want to leave our loved ones behind, or we still have things to do before we go, or simply we just don't want to go to an unknown place.

In my opinion, fear or discomfort about the word death is because it is a mysterious thing.

We do not know what is on the other side, and nobody ever lived to tell us.

In different religions, cultures, and folklore, there are various ideas about what happens when a person dies, but as I said earlier, we can't verify any of them. So, nobody knows what's on the other side. The stigma attached to death is so intense that nobody dares to think that something great can be waiting for them over there, thus the fear.

Anyone who is fighting a life-threatening illness does everything to get better, but it often happens that they are so beaten up by the sickness itself that the thought of giving up drifts in their mind many more times than it should.

How do I know that? For that, let me take a stroll down memory lane.

I'm lying in a hospital bed, where I have been quite a number of times over these past several years. I look to my right arm and see an IV pouring drops of fluids little by little into my arm. The normal saline mixed with the drug is so cold that it makes the entire hospital feel like an igloo. I look at my left arm and see another line going through my vein, just in case the nurses need immediate access. I've been through this drill plenty of times before.

This time my hospital stay is for about seven days until my antiepileptic drug levels reach the therapeutic window. I have a space cap on with a dozen electrodes sealed down to assess my brain waves and detect any subclinical seizures. The goal of my stay is to reduce my seizure medications from five down to four by switching to phenobarbital, a barbiturate that was synthesized one hundred years ago.

Another analog of this drug class is used in assisted suicide; hence I am here for constant monitoring.

I've had nearly five hundred seizures during the first year after my surgery. Fortunately, these have all been focal as opposed to generalized seizures.

You may think of generalized seizures as a person convulsing, but mine are not like that. I may or may not have an aura beforehand. When I do, I feel like someone is digging into my neck, sort of like someone is trying to choke me. And sometimes, my lips tingle.

Unfortunately, exercise is out of the question, as too much exertion can spark a seizure at any point. I've gone from someone who lifts every day to someone who must resort to yoga. These are some of the adjustments I've had to make.

My typical seizures have always been the same. They would present with my right lip twitching out of control for about sixty seconds, followed by a post-ictal period lasting a few minutes. My epileptologist and I have exhausted our complete arsenal of drugs. Frankly, he is probably tired of going through that. I'm the patient from epilepsy hell. I've gone through nearly ten seizure drugs, with most landing me in the hospital because of side effects. I am so desperate for a drug that works.

When a seizure occurs, it's another reminder of what I've been through since the surgery. There have been highs and lows with these seizures—highs for a drug that works at first, lows when it doesn't. I just keep chugging along.

On every visit to the hospital, I somehow managed a way to not let my employer know about the seizures for fear that they could infer I was unqualified or unfit for this role. I have a field position and never have to be in the office. . . thank God. So, I carry my laptop around all the time. Nevertheless, it's a good thing that my epileptologist warned me about the weeklong visit. I have to sneak in work for the whole week. . . with a very weak Wi-Fi signal. There is nothing else to do but write, eat, sleep, watch a movie, and have the technicians watch me defecate.

Asbestos is in the cafeteria this week, which means nasty food gets catered, and I miss out on their world-class macaroni and cheese.

I just lie in bed all day and count down the time until 5:30 a.m. when the medical team does their rounds. I spend most of the day thinking about smart questions to ask the attending physician to make their conversations with me last longer. Rarely do I get to speak with a doctor. Otherwise, the only other interactions are with my nurses, Christine and Kathy, who watch me pee into a plastic pan.

*   *   *

I look back at my life five years ago—before I ever had to worry about seizures. . . before my desperation to find the right combination of drugs. . . before all the hospital visits. . . before everything. I dream of the days when I didn't worry about anything except what clothes to wear to match my funky socks.

As it is said, life is what happens when we are busy making other plans. I have never thought about getting sick—I mean, not so severely sick. Like any ordinary person, I knew that we should be thankful for being healthy, but I don't really remember being too grateful for my body working normally in a healthy manner.

Perhaps it's human nature to appreciate things not when they happen, but when they are gone. Before my diagnosis, my biggest worries were my future plans and where I wanted to see my life in the coming five or ten years.

That's what any healthy person does, isn't it? But things began to change, and my body started to ask for my attention. We can ignore it until a certain time, as I undoubtedly did.

It all started when I noticed my speech changing. I can't exactly pinpoint when, but it was around the same time that I completed my pharmacy training and transitioned to my dream job. The pharmaceutical industry was my calling. It was my big break. So, I thought these changes were due to the stress and pressure of getting a new job and performing well in it. I had never experienced symptoms like these before. I used to dismiss them, thinking they would eventually pass.

## AGITATION

On my first day at the new job, I was excited while talking to my new manager and had so much I wanted to say. It is like when you have a lot of ideas in your head and try to write them down, but the words you manage to scribble are irrelevant and strange. The ideas that seem amazing in your head look disfigured and scattered on the paper. It was a lot like that, but I didn't realize it until I saw my manager staring at me as if I was not making any sense to her.

I paused for a moment, and then it hit me that what I had said hadn't come out right. It was high-pitched, and the words were muffled.

I knew I was expected to repeat myself, and I did, and the rest of the conversation went fine. Others would think it was a one-time thing, but not in my case. It got worse and worse as time moved on. I tried to brush it off as stress initially, but it transformed into something completely different and uglier.

Then it happened again while I was delivering a presentation to my colleagues. I tripped over the words. I would pardon myself and continue.

It seemed simple at first, and I could never have imagined where it would lead me. I also noticed that I was becoming increasingly obsessed with things. If something insignificant or trivial happened, I would think about it for a long time until it began to hurt my brain. I was not an obsessive person, so it was very unlike me.

After a few months, my speech wasn't getting any better. When I spoke, it was hard to get words out clearly. I began to mumble. It had gotten to the point where I noticed something was very wrong.

I felt agitated and helpless. It was as if I had so much to say, but somehow, my senses were not in control. Whenever I tried to speak, the words somehow struggled to set themselves.

I was attempting to distinguish if it was work-related at all. I relaxed on my bed. My brain was calm. Then I reached a meditative state. Slowly and clearly, I began to talk out loud. At first, I started with two- to three-word phrases. All checked out. Then I upped the word count. I repeated the same sentence over and over, but it sounded different each time. I thought that this might be psychological.

My voice still wasn't working fine the next day. Or the next. I became so angry that I punched a wall in my apartment. I hadn't done that since college when we purposely wrecked our ten-person house. We were drunk at the time. It was okay. Most of us got our security deposit back.

But this time, I was sober. It was uncharacteristic of me ever to get angry.

The slow, progressive slurring had only gotten worse. I asked my girlfriend, Maddie, "Does my voice sound bad?"

It was a question that I wanted an answer to. She could have said, "Yeah, it's terrible. You need to get checked out." But she refused to notice a change.

"I sound like an idiot." My voice was husky. I stopped short of breaking down.

"No, you don't. I cannot see any change. You are just fine." She kissed my forehead while giving me a warm smile. It did make me feel a bit better, but somehow, I was not convinced. I know she was trying to be kind. She did not want me to feel any less. Maddie was my confidant, though. No matter what, I trusted her above all else. Maybe I was crazy?

But no. This time I wasn't. I knew I had a problem. I knew my body best.

My friends had noticed the decline in speech when I asked them. They would sometimes comment aloud that they could hear it but said it wasn't that noticeable. These were people that I hung out with quite regularly, so of course, they would hear a change. I was torn between trusting my girlfriend or my friends. Regrettably, for some strange reason, my girlfriend won out.

I should have known at that point. It's the *Fulton luck* kicking in! When I say luck, it is bad luck. It is a beautiful, magnificent, delightful slice of glorious bad luck; no other bad luck exists in the universe quite like the Fulton's.

It may sound like a comical joke that exists in every family, but the *Fulton luck* is true. My sister, Sydney, and I joke about it because we know something bad will always happen in our happiest moments. It always comes at a time when you think life's too good to be true. Even the most terrible things are not exempt from the *Fulton luck*. Sydney should have sent out a warning when things were going well for me. Or I should have warned myself. God works in mysterious ways, but he didn't have to give me something to fear.

## JE T'AIME

While I was still figuring out what was happening to my speech delivery and voice, we took a trip to France. This wasn't my first time out of the United States, but it was a vacation where I could finally relax and not worry about my speech. I decided to leave my troubles behind for a little while. It was really for a work trip. . . but it was also a getaway for me and Maddie, one we really needed. The ten-day getaway was therapeutic. We flew into Lyon and traveled to the east side of France. We traveled to Riquewihr, known for its "Beauty and the Beast" style houses.

On the next stop, we found ourselves looking over Italy and Switzerland on the top of Mont-Blanc in Chamonix. We took a cruise down the Rhine River in Strasbourg. But we fell in love with Annecy. It had swans and a nude beach. It was surrounded by mountains and canoes on the lake. And the Pont de Amours—the "Bridge of Love." Our picture there still brings back good memories of that vacation.

In Paris, we did all the touristy things—the Louvre, Eiffel Tower, Notre Dame Cathedral, Palace of Versailles, and so on. But I most regret attending the Moulin Rouge. It was the last night before she left. I totally blew it. A stupid fight, and that was it. All the champagne and nude girls were dancing, and she didn't move her head the whole time. I did the "apologetic boyfriend" ordeal, and it didn't work. Nothing in my arsenal of apologies could calm Maddie down. Her face was red, and she wasn't talking to me. There's nothing worse than a girl being silent.

I had hoped we would fight it out like normal couples. But the truth is we never fought. I can't remember us getting mad at each other at all in the past. Sadly, I can't even remember what the fight was about. I was already in the doghouse. Our vacation ended with a lack of romance.

She left in the morning while I attended my work conference. Anxiety continued to build up over time. I couldn't wait to get home. I would take back those nine wonderful days in a heartbeat in exchange for that last night at the Moulin Rouge. France was the commemorative moment to the end of my perfect life.

I was greeted with a "What's gotten into you" as soon as I got home.

"I'm not right; somethings not right!" I said with aggression.

"Cleary not. I don't know, Joe. You have to get checked out."

"FINALLY!"

What the hell was I thinking all this time? I had noticed this speech issue all along and did nothing about it. I didn't need permission from anyone, including Maddie. I had a feeling the *Fulton luck* had crept in at an opportune moment to mess with my life. I needed to see a neurologist pronto to rule out everything or find something. I just wanted an answer to why I was like this.

The apartment felt empty even though Maddie was there. It was like stepping on eggshells around her. I was in zombie mode. I didn't do anything stupid before I spoke with a neurologist. It was a cold home, and I was nervous.

The night before my neurology appointment, I traveled to Matt's place. His family had a beach house. I had hoped it would relieve my anxiety. I drove with the window down and music obnoxiously blasting with the bass turned all the way up. I knew it would be empty and cool, unlike that summer, with baking temperatures and overly crowded beaches. Salty November air was what I needed. The smells of the sea got heavier as I traveled toward the beach. To feel a normal feeling felt nice.

His family's house was toward the end of the beach. The famous Kite Festival had just ended, but a few stragglers had elected to stay behind. There's no better site than kites on a beach with parents teaching their kids how to fly them. It was windy, but not too windy. The weather was just right. Matt came out to greet me with a smile.

"I can't believe you came all the way down here."

"Not a problem, plus I love driving."

"Head inside."

Matt gave me a tour of the house. His place was fit for ten people, though most had already left. All rental beach houses are nice, especially when you get closer to the water. His beach house was right on the sand.

He took me outside to say hello to his father, whom I had known for twenty years.

We started walking on the shoreline in no particular direction. The waves were already receding by then. There was a sandbar with a horseshoe crab, which I lifted and chucked back into the ocean. It was the perfect night for a long walk on the beach. We stopped to toss the football around a little bit before eventually sneaking into the nature preserve. When we climbed that hill, my emotions changed.

Everything changed. I had gone into a trance.

"What are those sandpiper birds doing? They know the water is only going to come back to the shore with those waves. Those birds are so dumb. They remind me of a pigeon. Only a dumber pigeon."

I gazed at the birds, watching them run back and forth. It was a mesmerizing feeling. I was in a daze. My head got light, and my feet didn't even touch the ground. All was numb as soon as I crossed that hill. It was like I was high on something. And it was not marijuana. I didn't even look at Matt. I just stared off into oblivion.

Besides my *stoned* moment, the conversation changed immediately to a very deep topic. I just snapped.

"There's something WRONG WITH ME! I swear there's something wrong. What the hell is wrong? It's not my vocal cords, so it's got to be in my head. What is it, Matt?"

I bent down and clutched my head into my arms. That was the pinnacle of desperation and an outcry for help. And there I was, asking a person who worked for the county for a medical diagnosis. Thank God I was going to find out what it was the next day. I prayed the neurologist would give me some kind of answer. Like, "Take this pill." One and done.

His dad asked me if I wanted to stay over, and I sure did. What better feeling than sitting in a long sleeve T-shirt as the sun goes down and spitting sunflower seeds into a bottle? But I had to go because reality was over. I had to face the music the next day. I was so pissed when I sat in that car to leave—no more perfect nights on the beach. I had to get back home.

The next day I arrived at the       main hospital. I was stepping into the main doors of the neurology department. I waited all this time to take a neurological exam. Not just the two hours in the waiting room but the seven months prior, complaining about my speech and doing nothing about it. But I was there, waiting and waiting until my name was called.

"Joseph Fulton," the receptionist shouted out to the packed office. She wanted my insurance. As soon as it was processed, I went back to the neurologist's office. I didn't know what he was going to say. His office was at the end of a long hallway, and to the right was the door.

When I got there, he didn't stand up to shake my hand. Instead, he got down to business by examining me.

*Okay, five items, do a bunch of stuff, then recite the words. What's today's date? Who's the president? Follow my finger. Smack your lips. Move your tongue back and forth. Blink real tight. Walk in a straight line like you're taking a sobriety test. The neurologist had nothing else for me to do, so I spoke up.*

"Doc, I know something's not wrong with me physically. But I'm slurring, and it's progressing."

"I don't know. It could be a lot of things."

"Is it multiple sclerosis? Seems like it could be."

"Listen, you are young and strong." I noticed he left out the healthy part.

He rattled off a bunch of things and his suspected diagnosis—Tourette syndrome. I think he made that up because he had to write something down for my visit, some kind of evaluation for his records. I didn't meet the criteria for Tourette syndrome. I didn't agree at all.

He sent me to get officially checked out and to cross off the name of diseases I potentially had. I acted pretty blasé about the entire thing. I felt differently. I was no longer anxious now that I knew I would get an answer. I was getting an MRI. A relaxed feeling came over me. So, I waited until the time had come.

I drove around looking for a meal spot. Lunch was at Applebee's. I had a burger listed on the QR code that I'd never seen before. Checked my watch. . . it was two hours before the MRI! Some people hate MRIs. I had to have one for my back surgery. But I was especially looking forward to this one. Taking my sweet time, the server was waiting for me to pay, get up, and leave. I couldn't blame him at all.

Two hours later. It felt like a lifetime had passed.

I went back to the hospital.

I waited some more.

## THE SHOCK

Now, this was interesting! Why are sperm counts decreasing worldwide? This was noteworthy news. I already knew it was because of lifestyle and environmental factors. Smoking is associated with all diseases known to man. Our chemical plants cause pollution, so the decrease in sperm counts may have something to do with the climate. I had to find out the link to what was affecting sperm counts.

Time had flown by as I was reading this article. I had to read fast because MRIs had a limited wait time. I was fascinated with the Time magazine article that lay beside me. I actually read through this article instead of pushing it aside and looking at pictures of a who-broke-up-with-who trashy magazine.

My name was finally called. Putting on a gown and slipping into those medical socks. . . I'm not too fond of those anti-slip crunchy socks. The MRI was peaceful yet stressful. The only anxiety I felt was that I had to keep my head still for an hour or risk messing up the scan. I didn't want any blurry images that came from not being as still as possible. I couldn't afford to screw this MRI up. I had to deal with the noises of rattling rocks, buzzes, and beeps of the machine. I knew it would all be over soon.

After the MRI, I felt a sigh of relief and had the results already in my hand as proof. The other copy of the scan had already been sent to the doctor. But what am I going to do with a disc... bingo.

I received a portable CD-ROM when I began my new job. I never thought that thing would come in handy. It was to be hooked up via the USB slot on the computer. Fifteen seconds passed before I had it all running—CD-ROM, disc, and USB. Now's the moment of truth, I thought while it was downloading. Images popped up. I worked in the neurology field, so I saw other people's scans. Enough to figure out...

"Oh shit."

I didn't know what it was, but it was something scary. The disc read "FULTON," so I knew it was my head. I waited hours to figure out what that was. I wondered if the neurologist got the copy at all... he was supposed to call me right away to tell me what that was, or maybe it was nothing at all. I was now grasping at straws not to believe what I saw.

I was trying to be rational here. But the irrational side of me kicked in. There was always a chance that the secretaries messed up and wrote "FULTON" on the wrong disc.

Or maybe that's just what Tourette syndrome looks like... I was so confused.

If the doctor was right, all I had to do was a little speech therapy and be on my way! And I do this ritual when I brush my teeth. That was it all along. Is this curable? Can you find Tourette syndrome on an MRI of that size? It didn't make sense that there was a mass. My mind was running wild.

Ring!

Dude, it's about time. I had waited about four hours for this call. I was hoping he would have a diagnosis for me.

"Hello, is this Joseph?"

"Yeah."

"This is your neurologist. There's a mass on your brain, and the radiologist can't tell if it's calcified. He can't tell if they have a fried egg appearance or not. It's probably DNET, so you won't have to worry. With DNET. . ."

I couldn't keep up with the medical jargon.

"So, is it like cancer?" Hoping he would just get to the point.

I imagine him thinking that I was in shock. And I was. Revealing the results of an MRI would naturally have this effect on anyone, good or bad. But I really had no idea what he was talking about. I needed an interpreter at this point. I couldn't understand. I hoped he'd just tell me if I should worry.

"Yeah, Joe, sorry. The radiologist thinks it's either DNET or some type of oligo. We need to figure out the pathology."

"Okay, what are those names? I'll do my research."

"DNET" stands for dysembryoplastic neuroepithelial tumor, or it can be either oligodendroglioma or oligoastrocytoma."

"Can you spell that?"

"D-y-s-e-m. . . can you repeat that?"

"We are going to send the radiology report over to the cancer center to decipher. I suggest you call them tomorrow."

The first thing I did when I hung up the phone was laugh. This tumor wasn't even close to the worst thing that has happened to me. It was just another thing. For the first couple of moments, I remember thinking how cool it was to have a brain tumor. None of my friends have that. Then I naturally snapped out of the fact that I could ever think that having a brain tumor was cool.

Any sane person would go straight to Google and search the prognosis of each of the tumors. DNET fine, oligo bad. And for the next while,

I sat, knowing only I knew about the tumor (besides the doctor and radiologist). Once I received that call, every single facet of my life would change.

I called Maddie.

"I WAS RIGHT!" I said to her with a little grin on my face and a sigh of relief. She was never wrong, but now she was. I was right for once, even if it meant me having a brain tumor to prove it. Satisfaction.

We spoke about what the plan was going forward. "I'll call the hospital tomorrow. You'll take a personal day off of work and join me at the appointment. We'll hear it's DNET, and I'll get speech therapy. I mean, but what if it's not? Alright, we'll just wait."

This was just another giant and scary moment. *Fulton luck* struck again! I felt a minor heart attack with the stress of the moment.

It took a while to calm down. I pray every night, but that night I skipped the prayer. It wasn't that I was mad at God or anything. I just needed to go to sleep so I didn't stress about all the crap that had been laid in my lap. I decided to deal with the stress in the morning.

I called on Thursday and got an appointment on Friday. That Friday was perfect because it gave me time to slow down at work. It also gave me time to overthink whatever diagnosis it may be. These frightening thoughts might have been just as bad as the tumor.

## TUMOR ON PAPER

The oncologist broke the news. I was stunned. It was not good. Why did it have to be a mix of oligos? I didn't even know what that meant at the time or how serious this was. So, this tumor will make my life hell until I kick the bucket? It could be worse, could be better. Oligo—whatever your name is, you are my hell right now.

"You could have had this for a decade by now. Most people are only diagnosed after a seizure," the oncologist said with confidence. "The reason you may not have noticed it is because of a thing called neuroplasticity."

My brain had essentially rewired itself to perform all necessary functions. Seeing the size of this tumor made complete sense. Every neuron would have to go around it. It altered my brain.

I have carried this rock around for ten years, and I just turned 28, so that means I could have had this since college or pharmacy school.

The oncologist told me that this tumor type was a slow-grower. At first, I was scared to learn about my tumor other than what the doctor told me. Nerves from such a diagnosis were more than I could take at this moment. But I built up the courage and became curious. I finally read the MRI report, which stated:

*"A mass lesion is identified mostly centered in the lateral aspect of the left precentral gyrus. There is a possible extension into the posterior-most aspect of the left middle frontal and inferior frontal gyri. In greatest axial dimensions, this measures 4.8 x 2.8 cm. This lesion appears in two radiographically distinct parts, one of which consists of significant thickening of the cortical (gray matter) surface. The second part fails to demonstrate mass effect (as opposed to the first part) and probably represents edema or encephalomalacia in the sub-adjacent white matter."*

All these details are how the tumor looks, but in a paper format. That was how they had explained it to the oncologist. I could make out most of the words in that report but had trouble piecing them all together. I thought about reading further and learning more about it. I had already gone this far.

As I skimmed through the report, the oncologist said, "Joseph, how about we schedule the surgery for Tuesday?"

Wow, she was going to operate within four days, and I would do the functional MRI the day before. I was so confused.

Everything was moving so fast. There was no time.

I have to tell my friends, call my boss, handle my affairs at work, and call human resources to tell them I am taking a leave of absence. I needed to have more time to process this.

I just heard about this thing. I didn't know it was going to be that fast.

Let me go to church a couple of times before the surgery.

"Ah, I forgot; I have a medical meeting," she said. "How about we push it off to the twenty-first?" I agreed as if I had a say in the matter. The oncologist made my day.

I had more time to cross the things off my list. But that meant more time to dwell on this. I always wonder if getting an MRI seven months sooner would have made a real difference if I was to have surgery anyway.

Maddie and I already had preset plans to see my sister that Friday night. We figured we would just tell her then. We were objective enough to keep our composure, even knowing she would not. She is. . . a little bit. . . dramatic.

The more wine you get in her, the less time you have to speak. So, I had to make it brief. I had to be direct and to the point. I had to be on my A-game for this conversation. I was practicing with Maddie what I would tell Sydney. You only get one shot to say "I have cancer" for the first time. On the way, I was so confident telling Sydney about my diagnosis. This was something a few days ago I did not even know I had. Maybe I was overconfident about it. Maybe it was just indifference. Maybe I should watch the road. Cinder Street, to Post, to West Hill, to 25 Grant Avenue.

I knocked on the door and was greeted by my four-year-old niece, seven-year-old nephew, a three-legged dog, and finally, a yell from my sister. We walked in and were welcomed with love and smiles.

Maddie and my sister talked a thousand miles an hour while I joined my brother-in-law on the couch, watching the basketball game in silence. I had to fight the kids from stealing my cellphone, but I eventually seized it back. It is great being the cool uncle who comes in, gets the children all riled up, and then can leave afterward. But first, I had to have the talk.

It wasn't long before my sister and I were at the table. I have no idea where the kids went, but obviously, I didn't want them to hear.

"What's up, bro?"

"I'm good. How's it hanging?"

"You said you wanted to talk about something."

"Uhm, yeah, how's your family?"

"Okay, I know you didn't drive forty minutes up here just to ask that. Tell me, what's up?"

My reaction was a combination of chickening out and awkwardness. Maddie was just sitting there, having me feel out of place. I was feeling the pressure. The longer I waited, the quieter it got. Just man up and tell her.

"I have brain cancer."

I started bawling. I strutted into that house, thinking I was going to be the rough and tough hero. I'm sure this news is hard to deliver to any loved one, no matter what age and cancer type. Sydney had me repeat that statement out of confusion. She thought I was joking around. But you do not joke around with that and start crying. Being ten years older than me, she could not imagine this happening to her baby brother.

I couldn't explain much about it other than what I was told. I didn't have time to sit back casually and look it up like a student studying for his medical boards. Sydney had so many questions. I had the same ones. She was crying. This literally just happened. I needed time to drop the tough guy persona and accept it.

I didn't stay long for fear that my niece and nephew would see their happy uncle with red eyes. Bryce came downstairs and thought my sister and I had gotten into a fight. That was the only time I left without shaking Bryce's hand. I imagine Bryce looking at my sister and asking, "What just happened?" as I closed the door.

That was my tough guy moment, and I blew it. Saying it out loud made it come to life. It made all the emotions more real. Now, my seven-year-old nephew who is turning thirteen this year was old enough to comprehend what was going on. I didn't want him to know what was going on; each of us didn't want him to know what's going on. He would never remember what I had come over to say that night.

My dad had more of a matter-of-fact tone. I started by saying, "Don't freak out." Only bad news can come after that.

I told him every piece of information that I had and what was going to happen next. I cannot fathom what it is like to hear your own son telling you that news. His voice sounded angry and terrified, but he kept it together better than I had expected. We don't call that much, so when we do, it is important.

The last time he was in the hospital was for a kidney stone fifteen years ago. He does not take any medications and is healthy as a bull. He was nearly retired at the time. How could he possibly comprehend one of the most devastating illnesses to happen to his own son?

I have never seen my dad cry, not at funerals, weddings, or anything. I have seen him with a temper, but that's it. I was more scared to tell him because we only spoke about sports and doing my taxes. Now I dropped a huge bomb on him. I felt so bad after that call, knowing that I definitely ruined the future he had for me. Probably shattered it. There's a big difference between telling siblings versus parents. Telling a parent crushes you way worse.

Over the next two days, Maddie and I called our friends to let them know what was going on. We bonded through our strange and funny personalities. This was the ultimate test. We took turns calling our closest friends and bet who would freak out and those who offered their condolences. The criers were the worst because we would end up sobbing on the phone with them.

All our calls ended with, "Don't tell anyone." This was difficult enough. I didn't want word to spread before my surgery.

A call I will never forget was to my manager. I called her, and she thought I was resigning. I broke the news. The terror in her voice came out. But it was all out of genuine love. Out of all the friends I had called, she made me cry the most. I straight up lost it.

This kept getting more real. The weeklong delay allowed us to learn more about the tumor. Maddie did most of the research since she worked in oncology and knew all the intricate details. I didn't understand them as much as she did. Having her by my side was a total blessing.

She had her shot at not being a caregiver. I tried to give her an *out* several times, but she refused. We could have broken up before she got too attached to the frightening tumor. She said she would not bail on me. I had a girl by my side who could prove she would be there in sickness and in health. I was already planning a proposal for that upcoming summer. I made a pact with myself that cancer couldn't stop me. If I could do it, I was going to try; if I couldn't, I would try, anyway. I wanted to live a life of normalcy.

## CALMING NERVES

"We're going to brain map you," the neurosurgeon told me. "That means you will perform several tasks. In association with those tasks, we can identify which locations to remove or not remove. Your tumor is surrounded by some very sensitive areas."

"So, what do I do? I don't follow."

"Our technician will come in. This should take thirty minutes. They'll show you a picture, and you say what it is. You will hear words and repeat sentences. This will help us poke around during your surgery. Then you'll wear a mask during the MRI. We will use that information to map your brain."

"Wait, I'm confused," I said with a squint in my eyes. "About what?" She looked at me like I was a prat.

"What is the purpose of the tasks? Can you just have me repeat words and wear the VR mask during the MRI? I don't see why you need both."

"Because you're going to be awake during the surgery. We need you to be familiar with these tasks so we can have a baseline."

My heart stopped. I didn't know this.

I'm not going to do that. Screw it.

When I first told her about the process, Maddie was fascinated by awake craniotomies. She mentioned a story where someone was playing the violin during brain surgery. "Okay, good for them. I'm still not doing it. . . fine, I'll do it. I have no other choice."

I took the hour-long MRI—which turned out to be three hours. They asked me to hold my head still. . . I can't even hold my head still for three hours while I'm sleeping. I was so scared of what was going to happen. Maybe I would mess up the brain mapping if I flinched my head and something went wrong during the surgery. The entire thing is a blur. That functional MRI was something I had purposely tried to wipe from my memory. I just wanted to get out of that machine.

That previous week's delay prepared me for what was going to happen. I knew everything a patient should know and maybe a little too much. I had to be mentally prepared for every single thing that could happen. I'd be on the Man's good side if I did my homework.

Kristin and John took Maddie and me to watch Thor the night before the surgery and gifted me a pricey pillow, already knowing I was not going to sleep that night. It was an okay movie. In its defense, I was thinking about the surgery the whole time.

I had to set my alarm to be up early the next morning. By 5:00 a.m., I was already wide awake. In fact, I did not sleep. I wore a college T-shirt for good luck and some gray sweatpants to the hospital. I got ready, only to be in a hospital gown an hour later.

I called an Uber, and it was only twenty minutes away. . . so I guess I was really going through with this. Couldn't turn back now. Maddie and I romantically held hands in the Uber, sharing earbuds and listening to Kanye West. I cannot remember the song as I was dealing with a wall of worries that seemed to be collapsing in on themselves. I hated when it was time to get out of the car. I wanted to get back in.

We were so scared that we didn't speak until we arrived at the hospital. I think Maddie was more nervous than I was.

Smocks and damn hospital socks. Never at twenty-eight years old did I think that would be my runway attire to get my skull cracked open. While on the stretcher, I didn't move my eyes away from Maddie. She was holding back tears as best as she could while I was praying that the neurosurgeon had a steady hand. They started wheeling me off as I slowly let go of Maddie's hand. The anesthesiologist came immediately to insert the needle into my veins.

Six people and the neurosurgeon huddled around me.

I asked the anesthesiologist if I could count down to ease my nerves the best way I could in that situation.

"Ten. . . nine. . . eight. . ."

## HEAVEN

I woke up to a "Hi, Joe." The neurosurgeon wanted to make sure she didn't cause any other damage while poking my brain to remove the tumor. My head was strapped down, with part of the right side of my skull lying against the operating table. We started the tasks after I came to. I was dizzy but ready.

"What is this picture?" I did not know who the person was asking me these questions. I had never seen her before. I was already anxious enough.

"A car."

I didn't know what had happened. I fell back asleep, thinking that was normal protocol. It turns out that was my first seizure. They woke me up again. I was confused.

"Joe, are you with us?"

She then started asking me to repeat short sentences. I got through a couple. Seizure.

I was getting tired of this. I wanted it to stop. The neurosurgeon tried again, except this time, I did not get an opportunity to do a task. The surgeon poked once more. I kept hearing the commotion, but I was too dizzy to understand. Then it happened. . . the most glorious seizure I've ever had. It was beautiful, seriously.

It felt like my head was falling gently on a pillow. The softest pillow ever. This was a moment that I will remember until I'm gone and probably after. All I could see was a bright-white color. Almost translucent. I do not think it was a "coming back from the afterlife" or an "I went to heaven" scenario. It was most likely the bright lights and anesthesia that caused this. I remember thinking, I am dying right now. This feels so peaceful. I had never experienced that feeling, but still, I loved it. That was the seizure that ended the surgery. It made me wish for heaven.

Afterward, I read the transcript: *"The patient had many seizures. Keppra was used. The neurosurgeon felt it unsafe to go any further."*

Okay, maybe she got most of it. The primary literature quotes the success of a brain surgery to be complete resection, >99%, >95%, >90%, and ≤90%.

She told me before the surgery, "I'll be aggressive." Not that aggressive! I thought to myself that she would get the entire thing. Well, I guess not, based on the transcript. Maybe she'll leave just a little, so I could be slightly pissed at her. As long as she gets >95% out, I'd be happy. I mean, in the worst-case scenario, she'd get >90% of the tumor out. The scare of having a tumor, the phone calls to friends and family, Kanye West at 5:00 a.m., and then heading to surgery wearing those socks, with the gorgeous girlfriend crying by my side. I couldn't believe that all these events were happening. They weren't supposed to.

Damn, how life can change in two weeks. It was the nightmare scenario that I had never expected. It had better be a >95% tumor resection.

I came to find out that it was much worse. I have no idea what I'm talking about regarding cancer resections and brain-related research... but I know a little about numbers to realize this was NOT a good number.

What were you doing inside my brain to screw it all up? Don't you do this all the time? You'll be going home to a nice, warm dinner. Maybe stuffed peppers or homemade chili or whatever the hell you're eating. You have to prepare for the next patient. Meanwhile, I have to deal with everything that comes with an unsuccessful brain surgery forever.

\* \* \*

I am a pharmacist specializing in neurology, so I frequently attend regional, national, and international conferences. I work for a pharmaceutical company that doesn't quite specialize in epilepsy, but I attend these sessions anyway when I'm at medical meetings. These presentations are done by the top epileptologists in the world. I converse with them after the session and lay out the list of drugs I am on due to epilepsy that I had developed from the surgery.

I wear them like a medal of honor stitched to my suit, representing I am invincible. I am proud of how tough I appear. A typical person with epilepsy wouldn't be on more than two, yet I'm on over twice the number. A side effect of these drugs is slowing down our brain's neuronal firing. My job involves learning and presenting medical information, making it much harder for a slow brain.

"I'm surprised you're even awake," one epileptologist told me with a double take.

Yeah, no shit.

I'm on five drugs. Every hour of every day felt like I was about to fall asleep. Can you imagine how good of a job I could do if I were one hundred percent? I'd be the world's best industry pharmacist. Hands down.

The seizures have become more of an annoyance by now. I'm still conscious and fully aware when I have them. It's just embarrassing when I have them in front of people in social situations.

When I have a seizure, it's a brief reminder that I have a brain tumor just casually sitting up in my head. I wake up every single morning at seven o'clock and take my medications. Then I do the same thing at seven in the evening. I hope phenobarbital works because it's one of the few options before VNS.

My last surgery is something I don't want to go through again. The statistics say it's inevitable that I'll have another craniotomy if this thing grows back. I pray it never will. When you're positive enough, the situation becomes true. That's how I try to approach things, combatting the *Fulton luck*.

I can't count how many seizures have occurred by now. A great week was only having five focal seizures, whereas a bad week was having ten. It sounds dramatic, but it's true. The saddest part was these seizures had taken away two things that mattered the most: driving and speech. I needed those, and this tumor had taken them away from me. I miss driving the most. The seizures are the culprit. I resorted to getting that feeling by driving around inside my apartment garage.

Driving had allowed me the freedom to just get away from everything. I would drive anywhere, however long the distance is, while blasting music or listening to a true crime podcast and reflecting on the day. Driving late at night with a buzz is the most beautiful thing because there is no rush to be anywhere. A car is a sacred thing that invokes many good and bad memories. It can be a beautiful box.

I remember driving over the bridge when I learned Michael Jackson had died. I remember driving after the bars closed with my friend James to get McDonald's. I remember breaking up with my college girlfriend overlooking the city while a cop knocked on my side window, thinking we were up to no good. He interrupted the "it's not you, it's me" speech.

And I have memories of driving in my godfather's car. He'd drive me all the way to the racetrack to place bets. I would place show bets to win twenty cents, and he would bet the two favorites in an exacta and always lose. I inherited his 1999 gray Crown Victoria when he passed away. There was a horseshoe in the back of that car under the rear window. Those memories I keep in that horseshoe. And those refractory seizures from a botched surgery took that away from me. The neurosurgeon messed up, and because of this, the seizures will never go away.

Trips I used to take to my girlfriend's apartment, to driving up an hour to see my sister and her family, then back down two hours to visit my dad—they were all gone. Uber became my best friend and a huge amount of my expenses. If I wanted to hang out with my friend who lived all the way out in the countryside, that would cost me $45 one way. That is a huge amount for someone who can never afford to pay the rent and student loan debt simultaneously. I had to get my blood drawn weekly for a year, and an Uber would cost me $7 to get to LabCorp. The only benefit from this was the five stars I received, which is sad.

Having a slow brain from all the seizure medications and speech difficulties makes it nearly impossible to give a decent presentation. I present medical data to doctors for a living. It sounds like a sales representative role, but it's not. . . it's not something I can describe, and who cares anyway. I am still going to speech therapy twice a week. Watching old videos of me confidently giving seminars to hundreds of people is amazing. But now, I still have trouble completing a full sentence. Imagine thinking of a word, and all that comes out is slurring and mumbling. Or nothing at all.

Never take anything for granted, as some people do their entire life. I could never expect my life to go from content to looking like a wired-up alien within five years as I do now in this hospital bed. There are always those that have it way worse. I'm still grateful to be alive. I'm making the best of the situation. And I still can charm Christine and Kathy—my temporary girlfriends in room 818.

# CHAPTER 2:

# DEALING WITH THE DEVIL

My eyes stung as I struggled to open them, so I shut them tightly. A few moments later, I tried again, hoping it would be different, a little easier this time. Effort after effort, I managed to open my eyes, but it drained me of all my energy.

I was alive, but barely.

A wave of nausea followed by vertigo hit me while I lay still. Taking a deep breath, I focused on keeping my eyes open and instantly wished I hadn't woken up.

Breath after breath, my body felt lighter, as if I were floating. I became so content laying on that comfy pillow that I could've died right there and been okay with that. Yet, I could sense that it was bad news from then onward. Based on the number of seizures I had, I could tell I was not doing well. . . or the neurosurgeon did not do well. So, I mustered up the courage to ask what I already suspected.

"How did we do?" I was terrified of the response I received. It would not have been good. I wish she had never told me.

She had somewhat of a calming but guilty voice. "Forty percent. You just need to rest." Just forty percent?

They had a reason for it. It was initially planned as a five-hour-long surgery, as I was told by the team of doctors, but I started having seizures after one and a half hours on the table, so naturally, it had to be cut short. It was what it was.

Then I passed out again.

After what felt like a moment or perhaps a century, a voice came out of nowhere, dragging me back to reality. "You have a lot of visitors to see you," said the nurse pushing the hospital gurney I was being wheeled out on.

But I had other things on my mind. Therefore, I asked the nurse again, "How much did she get out?"

I was deeply afraid that she knew or that forty percent was just a guestimate.

"About forty percent," the nurse replied. I had two confirmations on the number now.

She paused for a moment and gauged my reaction. She realized I wasn't thrilled.

"You have about ten people waiting for you. We usually only allow two or three, but we made an exception for you."

I didn't say anything but felt a tornado of wild thoughts in my head.

*Is it a pity reception because the surgery had gone so wrong?*

*Or is it a welcoming reception because the hospital staff was very friendly?*

*Or is it an "All these people came to see you, so we let them in, but they have only a few minutes?"*

It hurt my head a little more. I was experiencing many emotions all at once and felt deeply about each. At the same time, my mind was foggy, too. I wondered if that was how everyone going through a craniotomy felt. My brain was very inflamed. Rational thoughts faded in and out.

Getting wheeled out was so awkward. As I came out, I received a lot of blank stares and wary expressions. They didn't know what to say or how to greet me. They also didn't realize that I was fully doped with an enormous cap around my head that looked like something from the Coneheads.

"Only forty percent," was what I could say to them. But they already knew before I got there. A nurse who had been in the operating room had told them with chagrin. They expected I wouldn't be happy. That probably was the reason they let them all in.

I had the feeling of a circus animal with all those eyes staring at me. I was too broken by the outcome to feel relieved. So sad that the emotion of anger was no longer possible at that point. So desperate at the moment.

Sydney, Bryce, and my dad were there. They couldn't even put on a fake smile. Sydney's eyes were red from crying, Bryce looked uncomfortable just being in a hospital, and my dad was jittery. The others were Kristen, John, and Maddie's clan. Maddie's own mother probably took it harder than anyone besides my girlfriend. Maddie climbed on my bed to hold my hand, making me feel that I had all the support I needed. The next thing that came up was my dad quizzing me with sports trivia.

"Who's the Eagles quarterback?" I used all of my brain cells. "Carson. . . We. . . We. . . Wentz." That was typical of him. Only he would say something like that.

"When did they last win the Super Bowl?"

"Never."

"See, he's going to be fine." He shrugged as he looked at nobody in particular.

I would have found that hilarious if my brain didn't feel like scrambled eggs. Now I wonder, was it for the others, or was it an attempt to make himself feel a little less worried about me? Everyone was trying their best to diffuse the tension in the air. I couldn't shake the sense of guilt that I was the one who had cancer, that I put them through this, that I had hurt them this badly.

It's a repetitive cycle. The guilt overtakes me, and in turn, they feel helpless. By feeling helpless there was nothing in the world that could change what I just went through.

Then out of nowhere, this guy in blue scrubs came up to us wearing a funny hat and guitar, which wasn't funny at all, considering how much I was hurting. I didn't want to look at him, so I just held Maddie's hand firmer.

The guy said, "You get two songs."

It was irritable; I did nothing but blink at him. But the thoughts in my mind were aggravated.

What the heck? You're wasting minutes being with my friends and family. I noticed he had an *MD* listed after his name. Even worse. He took the *bedside manner* piece a little too far. But then, in the next breath, I remembered something.

Oh yeah, why not have him sing happy birthday to my girlfriend? It was a pretty dick move to have brain surgery one day before Maddie's birthday. So, why not make use of this opportunity?

He began singing. It all felt good for once. I was still in pain, but at least Maddie was smiling. The moment was beautiful; remembering her birthday immediately after brain surgery was also a suave move. My second song was Stairway to Heaven, just to be an ass and see him struggle. He fumbled. Probably not good Karma. At least the neurosurgeon had left that part of my twisted personality in.

Completely missed the tumor, but the humor remained intact.

I shifted in bed uncomfortably once the song was over. Now, get out. Ouch. I needed medicine badly. The pain started setting in as the drugs started wearing off. My memory is hazy after that. I was mostly in and out, but one thing was constant: pain.

As soon as they wheeled me off, puke came out. Waterfalls of puke.

"It's all right," the nurses said. They were talking to me like I was a baby. At that point, I had to be treated like one, too. I had never been so physically useless. Nurses were cleaning me off until I got up to my room.

I begged for water, but they knew I'd regurgitate it all out. All I received was a small cup of ice chips. That was good for now. As I twisted and turned, writhing in pain, I accidentally hit a tube. It was connected to me.

A thing that makes every man quiver. The catheter.

The ice chips came out with the puke.

Seizure after seizure. The nurses didn't know what to do besides infuse Keppra, clean up drool, and continue to wait for changes in treatment.

My body was under attack by something I couldn't see or control. I was new to the whole seizure thing, so whenever I felt one coming on, I could only just bang on the nearest fixture. I couldn't scream out loud because words didn't come out. It seemed like the nurses came into the room every thirty minutes to make sure I hadn't done harm. My brain couldn't differentiate a seizure from what may be happening inside my brain. Was something else going on? I often wondered, is this normal?

The neurosurgeon initially told me I would be out of the hospital in three days. That would be a hell of a recovery if that were true. But I knew I wouldn't leave the walls outside of the hospital room for a while. I was a prisoner with no set sentence.

Maddie slept in the hospital for the next few days, including her birthday, soaked in tears. After visiting hours, the nurses let her sleep in the uncomfortable hospital chair and waiting room. She was really good to me. She did not deserve this. At that point, she transitioned into my caregiver, who I depended on above all else. It was not fair. I was in and out of consciousness, but she was always there each time I opened my eyes. She would always fetch anything that I needed; meanwhile, I was completely helpless on my own.

Moving was exhausting. My muscles were weak and lazy from the painkillers. I did as much as I could from bed. But those nurses were heroes. They did most things for me. Having someone brush your teeth for you is one thing, but using a bathroom pan is demeaning.

I was already pee shy. When they removed the catheter, I strained. I couldn't leave unless I moved my bowels occasionally. So much Colace and MiraLAX. A confirmation that there was no chance I was getting out of there anytime soon.

The doctors did their rounds daily and before the crack of dawn. I couldn't comprehend anything they were saying. This is how the conversation went:

"Good morning, Joseph." Was that a question? Or a statement? I didn't know who this was. Oh, a doctor. Okay, got it.

"I'm going to ask you some simple questions. It's part of a neurological exam."

I immediately forgot who he was talking to. Me? Oh, right. He was facing me. Speaking crystal clear. But my eyes drifted off. I closed them. Immediately, I forgot what he looked like. The next thing I knew, I saw a bright light shining into my eyes. It was from a cellphone.

"He has second-degree nystagmus in his left eye," he muttered to the team behind him. I didn't see them walk in. What were they doing here?

"Repeat after me." Okay, I got this. "It's a sunny day outside." Already forgot the question. Or the statement. Crap, this is hard.

"Who is our president?"

"It's either Obama or Trump," I said. But why would I know the name Trump if he was already president? I had no shot at getting these correct, but remembering the question was a step in the right direction!

"Recite these three words back to me. Orange, tree, cat." Immediately forgot the instructions.

I got immensely frustrated. I've been a perfectionist all my life. Being hypercritical of myself is not a good thing when asked such simple questions... or statements. I don't know what I was being told to do.

They chose to dumb it down for me.

"What is your name?"

"Maddie!" I finally got one right. Or so I thought.

My dad had me set our fantasy football lineup, and I couldn't figure it out. Turning on the television was such a confusing task. I couldn't understand text messages. I watched videos of my friends wishing me well. I could hardly speak. It was so much more than I was ever prepared for.

I was struggling every day, even with the basic stuff. I was in the hospital for a week before doctors decided to release me. I was still having seizures, but they allowed me to go home anyway.

Hope is all I had left. Clinging on to any bit of it. I began to not believe in prayer anymore. No matter how much I prayed or people prayed for me, it wasn't working.

## PEACE OUT

The first meal I had at home was Taco Bell. It was a relief to have actual (fast) food. . . as opposed to hospital food. I ordered two of everything. Chalupas, quesadillas, nachos, hard and soft tacos. I didn't care that I ran up a bill for over $70. . . which is the equivalent of four to five mixed drinks in the city.

The bed was so comfortable. No more Lovenox shots or pulsations to prevent skin ulcers. Just a warm down comforter and Kristen and John's soft feather pillow. That was the first stage of relief I had felt in a while. The act of laying down on an actual bed from the past week of hell felt like heaven to me. I had no obligation to ever leave the bed. As soon as I closed my eyes to take a nap, crumbs were all over the bed from the tacos. I didn't care. Once I woke up, my mind started racing again. Reflecting on what the hell I just went through.

I wish I could remember more about the hospital. But then again, I don't want to. All I know is that the whole surgery was a big failure, and I was never the same.

But then again, who is?

If you walk up to a cancer patient, they will tell you a lot about the before and after experiences they learned from their diagnosis.

It's okay to suffer. By suffering, you can relate to someone else's suffering.

Silver linings.

If I were speaking to another brain cancer patient, I would have no problem telling them my story because we can relate to that common experience. Nobody asks me about my brain tumor, not realizing I'm itching for the question. But how would they know that? Overcoming adversity can be good, maybe not from cancer, but to have something relatable with others.

There's nothing wrong with bonding with someone on a deeper level. I've witnessed the most personal conversations that would have never happened except for similar tragedies.

A lesson I've learned from being in the hospital was how to be patient. That I would eventually get out of this place. It was going to be a long road back for me. Unfortunately, that is not everyone's.

Not everything comes back to normal. For both cured and not cured, the appreciation for life is there. There's something there. Even though the special value of life may be unappreciated, it's still there. In my conversations with most cancer patients, they undoubtedly have had some "Why me?" moments.

While recovering at home, I mistakenly believed the brain would heal much faster than I had initially thought. I couldn't read, write, speak, or comprehend anything. The only thing I was capable of doing was watching 90 Day Fiancé. The agony from the scar was intense, but I am the type who doesn't take his own pain medication. I am noncompliant with pain, sort of masochistic. I like the ability to sense all that I can feel. But even then, I was pushing the limits.

I don't know how long I spent recovering before my prognosis day came along. It must've been close to two weeks as far as I can remember. At the time, Maddie researched a head-to-head trial against PCV (a chemotherapy regimen) with or without radiation. They both had a survival rate of fourteen years. Would mine be worse? These are the unanswered thoughts I still don't know.

What if it wasn't oligodendroglioma at all? Would that count if I had already lived with this tumor for ten or fifteen years? What if it was glioblastoma?

I feel for the patients who have glioblastoma.

I read about this young teen who tragically died within thirty hours after a glioblastoma diagnosis. When she died, her sister found a note while cleaning out her closet: "Work hard, be nice, and give compliments."

She was so right. We should do this every day. There are some days I slack off. I have moments when I'm crabby. There are some days when I want to ignore people. I dismiss common courtesy like saying "please" and "thank you," and I think about what an ass I'm being.

It's amazing what a thirteen-year-old girl can teach you. Sometimes we all have to do a little better.

# P-D A Y

No matter what the neurosurgeon told me about my prognosis, I knew I would cry. If it was six months, one year. . . five, ten, twenty, forty. . . I would still cry. All the same, people that were in the hospital on the day of the surgery came in person for the revealing of my prognosis. They were all crammed up in the waiting room.

My heart was beating relentlessly, and I had already scouted out an empty room to cry after she gave me the number.

The neurosurgeon walked in with an uneasy smirk on her face. I needed her to get to the point instead of saying sentences no one understood. She gave me nothing of substance.

Okay, but what is my prognosis? I thought. Isn't that why you called this meeting?

"It's hard to say," she said.

What did this even mean? She was a doctor; wasn't she supposed to know?

"Like, what are the indicators?"

"You have great mutations," she said.

The only reason I knew these terms was that Maddie looked them up. I knew that having these were good: 1p/19q codeletion, MGMT, and IDH1. Not having all of these was bad. The neurosurgeon said all of them were present. I was happy so far.

Ahh, I should ask about how long I'm going to live.

Before I could say anything, Sydney interjected. "So, how long does he have to live?"

Choice words, Sydney. But it was what everyone was thinking. I was thinking that, too, but I had never heard anyone say it aloud. It gave me the chills.

"We don't actually know," the neurosurgeon said. "But it's an oligo, right?"

"All these terms blend together."

I felt helpless and furious at the same time. There was no answer to this, which my family and Maddie all came down here to know. At least let's have a discussion about this. But that was it. I thought she would address our concerns. I was so stunned that I had no more questions. She was just going to give me that. It was the classic "six months, one year" bit. I was someone else's problem now.

"You are better off asking a neuro-oncologist about this," she said while backing up toward the door. I took this as an escape route to my cry room. I cried over the unknown. Everyone needs a good cry sometimes.

And that was it. I got my answer. No answer at all.

## I'M LUCKY

The next thing I knew, I was relieving myself in a plastic cup. It was not for a drug test and was the grossest thing.

I touched every single thing that's already been touched, including the twenty-second floor elevator button. Gross. I signed-in and kept my eyes down. Then waited for a "Fulton!" call to enter the back room.

"Enter room 3."

*Welp, let's get this over with and get out.* The metal bench, a magazine if necessary, and a cup. Give it to the technician on your way out. I must have washed my hands five times, even more than that at the height of the COVID-19 pandemic. I sanitized myself over and over until I left that building. But this is a real-life thing. This is what you do for people who want to start a family. This is one of the reasons for the sperm shortage that I read about in the Time magazine article. I finally figured it out.

After getting this out of the way, I got three opinions from three different neuro-oncologists. I'm indecisive as it is, but these doctors are the ones who are responsible for my care. Sometimes the doctors encourage you to get another opinion if their ego doesn't get in the way. This step is so important. If it's a major decision and a debilitating disease, don't just listen to the first doctor.

The way I like to think about it is that you are just one out of a million patients he or she must see. In my field of work, I see each patient meet with the doctor for ten minutes at a time. All because they had to prepare for the next patient.

That doctor probably sees fifteen patients a day. No matter how smart they are, they tend to have different styles of treatment, and you must go with the one you trust the most.

It's also important that you take care of yourself during the period you are under treatment. Feel free to stand up for yourself and disagree if you need to. That's the approach that I took with my doctors.

There were two options: watch and wait, or go with radiation and chemotherapy. I presented my rationale with evidence. My speech impairment was only progressing, even with the surgery. What went from the option to *watch-and-wait* had gone to *we have to treat now*. I was genuinely excited. I expected to go through hell, but shrinking this puppy sounded more exciting. I wanted the treatment route. If anything were to happen, I could accept it as my choice.

Reflecting on this, I literally put my fate into another person's hands. I strolled into my neuro-oncologist's office with a backward hat and acted like I knew all the options that were available. I didn't have as much knowledge as I do now.

The amount of research going into finding a treatment for this disease is amazing, but not enough. It turns out I know literally nothing about my oligo and these doctors do. I guess that's what they get paid to do, just as I get paid to be an expert in what I do. This is a quick reminder to not act cocky when you don't know anything about oligos.

I was confident in my heyday, well, twenty-eight. But I was the youngest person in the waiting room. This humbled me, or it didn't. I was jealous. I secretly hoped that I saw a person younger than me that had cancer. I am so guilty of this. I mean, how messed up can a person be for thinking this way? Why does everyone live their life without a brain tumor but me? Why me? Does it remind us of suffering, that we are not alone? I go back to this a lot. I just want a normal life, but I remind myself that other people have invisible problems we can't see. Each of us is struggling with something or another. Some choose to show it, while others suffer in silence. Nobody's living a perfect, problem-free life.

I don't have to envy that now because I see it from the other side. How blessed am I to see thirty-three. Other people don't have that chance. I have had talks with friends about this.

If you watch the news, you'll see people die younger than me. Look at Sandy Hook, where these children don't even have a chance to grow up and do something great. All the time, notifications flash up on my phone: a bus full of college students hit a bridge; a seventeen-year-old was murdered, and the suspect is in custody; three juveniles drowned while swimming. Here I am complaining about living to thirty-three.

I hope no one has cancer. I've never been to a pediatric cancer center. That would probably straighten me out. I had much to learn about being a cancer patient. Here I am, under two months out from my diagnosis, and calling my own shots.

## CHOCOLATE AND CANCER CARDS

Perception and how we look at things change a lot. This is one of the biggest lessons I have learned through my prolonged sickness.

So, the word had spread, and people had already found out about my diagnosis. All my friends and their families. Gift baskets filled the island in the kitchen. Most of them were fruit baskets, so, unfortunately, lots of them got tossed. The chocolates remained intact. I had received what seemed like an endless number of cards per day. I noticed that they were not those generic Get Well Soon cards. The messages were thoughtful.

Cards mean a lot to me. . . . a trait I have picked up from Sydney. I always kept a stack of blank cards in my car and Forever Stamps in my wallet. Words mean the most to me. They live on forever.

I was randomly cleaning out the closet in my office last week and found a bundle of those *cancer cards*. It was nice to ponder over them and simultaneously to see who my friends were then and now. Those words. They were cathartic to me.

My Instagram direct messages were filled with kind messages. There were also messages from some people who I wouldn't expect cared that much about me. But the most meaningful were from people battling cancer whom I had known for a long time.

I received a text one night from an unknown number asking if it was me. This person told me she had leukemia and was cured. I was baffled. I knew her at the same time she was facing this terrible disease. You could find no flaws in her work. She was a regular girl doing regular things that people do. She would come out for happy hours and things of the sort. Meanwhile, she was battling cancer no one knew about.

And then I found out that a close friend had a brain tumor all along. She was diagnosed at age sixteen with a benign type of tumor. She still gets MRIs on occasion. Friends kept opening up to me now that they knew I was diagnosed. They wanted to share their stories with me. It was one of the few times I learned to shut up and listen.

I was in awe of their bravery in what they went through. It wasn't like a "rah-rah, go Joe" type. It was about the pains, the struggle, the anguish, and I needed that. I didn't want it to be all positive. I hated that "you're going to beat this" nonsense.

No, someone tell me how it is. Tell me that having cancer fucking sucks.

I needed to hear this from someone who could relate.

Although I appreciated the cards and gifts, it was a supportive push more than anything. And it was a lovely gesture. Truly, I am thankful for everything people sent me, but I was desperate for guidance. I didn't have the "bravery" aspect. I'm not a hero. I would rather choose NOT to have a tumor, and everyone can take back the "hero" thing.

Heroes are those who choose to do something—like enlisting in the military or becoming the 9/11 firefighters who run back into the buildings.

Listen, I did not want this. . . and suddenly, I was the hero? Jaclyn's friend told me one time, "You're a hero in how you handled it." I guess when you're put through crap, you have to find a way out.


## TREATMENT

Radiation was the best time I've had during this whole process. I'd meet Kristen at the train, which meant we were now riding buddies—she had to work, and I had to get my radiation. Coincidentally, our hospitals were right next to each other. She was the perfect buddy to complain about how cold that January winter was.

I felt horrible about how the surgery went, so I got redemption to shrink that tumor some more. The only thing wrong with radiation is it's known to affect your cognition in the long term. But I wasn't thinking about that. It was the short term for me. I wanted to get back to a life without cancer defining who I was and what I wanted to be. Radiation was my chance to get as much as I could to defeat the tumor that sat inside my skull.

My radiology guys were the coolest. The same three guys were with me five days a week for five weeks. They'd lay me down, crack some jokes, put my mask on, crack more jokes, ask what playlist I wanted on, and it was a chance to nap from the early wake-up call. Twenty-five sessions went by, and I never ran out of artists. Somedays, it was Green Day. On other occasions, we were playing Third Eye Blind. What's wrong with Alanis Morissette or a bit of Miley Cyrus?

You could do whatever you please in that radiation room. No one could judge or stop me. It was my temporary home, even though it lasted for twenty minutes.

Before my surgery, the tumor was 55.4 cm3, and after the radiation it shrunk to 33.4 cm3 on the volumetric report. It fell by 22 cm3! Glorious. I was feeling better. I was on steroids to reduce the inflammation from the surgery, but overall, my spirits were up. Something great finally went in my favor. I took the mask that they used to hold my head down. I carried that thing home as a sign of victory. My first victory. Treatment was off to a good start. Those were the good days before chemotherapy.

Please give me the hardest and most brutal one you got. Cancer ruined my life, so now I was going to ruin it. Yeah, positivity. I knew I could handle anything.

## STUBBORN

"Joe, we have Temodar, which is a good and safe drug. Most patients have little to no symptoms," I heard my neuro-oncologist say.

Wait, how did this move so fast? Okay, here we go; it's all a part of the plan. Thoughts were running through my head. It was here. Time was now.

"What else do you got, Doc?"

"There are more options available."

He gave me the very short list to choose from.

"Temodar is safe and the way to go. We also have PCV, but it's a dirty drug. It's a combination of procarbazine, lomustine, and vincristine."

"I think I can handle that. Doesn't seem that hard." I kind of knew the symptoms of chemotherapy. You throw up in the mornings. You lose some weight. That's what I thought the only symptoms would be. Easy.

"Go with the Temodar."

"PCV sounds fine."

The neuro-oncologist looked annoyed at me. "PCV is a 90's drug. Why not go with Temodar? It's much safer than PCV. They both have the same efficacy."

I'm stubborn. When I make up my mind, it's got to be done my way. Maybe if my surgery were successful, I'd be more likely to try Temodar. But that forty percent still got to me and I opted to take PCV.

I wanted to push my limits even if it meant I would regret it. I was twenty-eight. Most of these patients develop this cancer in their mid-fifties to eighties. If they used to go on this before Temodar existed, so could I.

Those cancer patients who suffer day by day on chemotherapy have it worse than me. I wanted to feel as close as possible to their suffering. I kept that in mind when making my decision. Why am I so *lucky* to have this type of cancer?

I once spoke to a man with non–small-cell lung cancer who was eight years out from his diagnosis. Not many people make it that far. I suspect that the reason is support, faith, and science. He has been on much rougher chemotherapy. Probably multiple times. I was willing to opt for the harder stuff. Temodar is a great drug, but I'm just crazy. "Yes, Doc. PCV."

I was going back to work at the same time, so I expected it to be tough to juggle chemotherapy and work. There was a much larger difference in pay from short-term to long-term disability when I hit three months. I was broke and needed the money. Just as I hit the three-month mark, I was back. I was hurting but fierce. In hindsight, I was not ready to go back. That was before my first round of chemotherapy. I could quickly see why people don't take PCV anymore.

## SET GOALS

Three days before my surgery in November, my friends took me to a bas-ketball game. I had a chat with my friend about doing something big after.

"It's a waste of brain surgery if you don't do something epic," he said. He was right, so I made a list:

1. Go to Greece

2. Visit my sister once a month

3. Hike more often

4. Go to Mass

5. Date night on Thursdays

6. Get back in shape

And on and on. But there wasn't something epic enough on there.

I can't free-solo on a mountain. I couldn't jump out of an airplane...
I mean, technically, I could. Eh, that's more of a bucket list item. I got it.
I'll run! It was safe on the ground, and I could just go slower if I wanted.
It was a perfect idea. It was kind of cliché and what many cancer survivors do. It was extremely motivating, and I could do a race by myself or with friends too.

I had only run a mile once and had been gasping for air. It was for gym class in high school.

I didn't run. Didn't have an interest. I lifted. I should have done a little more cardio. I guess running qualified as something epic.

Go big or go home. Push the limits of my capabilities. I was still hyper from the steroids, so instead of sleeping one night, I decided to write this:

> I cannot put into words my gratitude for the love and sup-
> port you have shown me through this difficult time in my life.
> However, I can assure you it was greatly appreciated from the
> bottom of my heart.
>
> Okay, enough with the mushy stuff. The primary outcome
> I've gained from all of this is a new perspective on life. Every
> single person has their own battles to face and overcome—be
> it physical, mental, or both. Rough patches will be encountered

*by everyone at some point. I am in no way special because of all this, and certainly not exempt.*

*As you know, I am a pharmacist by profession and was naturally drawn to neurology. Beginning my industry career, I had the opportunity to work with and for patients with neurological diseases. Throughout my time there, I met patients personally afflicted with these diseases. I learned that showing passion for the patient is one of the most important things you can do to impact their life. I wanted to continue that devout passion for patients facing neurological diseases, and so my journey led me to this company. I was given the opportunity to work alongside the most wonderful people. Little did I know that shortly after, I would be faced with my biggest challenge yet. This time, I would be able to fully comprehend the struggle from a patient's point of view.*

*Reality really slapped me in the face with this one. Before this, I considered myself a relatively healthy man with an excellent golf swing. My only personal health issue came from a high school football injury in 2005, where I had a lumbar discectomy from two herniated discs in my lower spine. I still regret not making that tackle, but no big deal. I learned how to cope and adjust. Now at the age of twenty-eight, I discovered I have a baseball-size primary brain tumor. Only several days before learning of the tumor, I underwent an awake craniotomy. I have now started radiation and will soon start chemotherapy for a combined total of fifty-eight weeks.*

*Many of you have heard me say this over the past couple of months: "serenity, acceptance, and courage." These few special words are a reminder for me to stay present, be positive, and overall maintain hope. You also keep me going. I have never felt this much love and support from my family, friends, colleagues, and, most importantly, my loving girlfriend. Maddie works in oncology, and I work in neurology. Neuro-oncology should be a piece of cake.*

*One thing many of you know about me is that I am also extremely stubborn. I am of Italian-Irish heritage and from a rough city, so I guess it naturally comes with the territory. And I will fight the living hell out of this thing. Mainly because—did I mention—I'm extremely stubborn?*

*Over the past couple of months, Maddie and I have been intensely researching brain cancers to understand better what the future holds. Unfortunately, there is an overall limited amount of treatment options available for patients. For the specific type of brain cancer that I have, including key genetic mutations, there is currently one Phase I clinical trial of which I screen failed, one closed Phase II clinical trial (which I am ineligible for anyway), and no other ongoing clinical research. Realizing how sparse research is sparked our desire to raise money specifically for the American Brain Tumor Association (ABTA), the first national nonprofit organization dedicated solely to brain tumors.*

*Their mission is to advance the understanding and treatment of brain tumors with the goal of improving, extending, and ultimately saving the lives of those impacted by a brain tumor diagnosis. Funding helps provide hope for the other 700,000 patients in the U.S. diagnosed with brain tumors.*

*Maddie and I have decided to run the Chicago Marathon in October 2018 to raise money for the ABTA. Our goal is to raise over $1,500. I was actively training and signed up for a half-marathon this April in anticipation of Chicago. Mind you, I despise running, but I love a good challenge. My stubbornness is apparently catching up to me. Fortunately, I have been medically cleared by the doctor to run. 26.2 miles will be no easy feat* *(especially during chemotherapy), but with love and encouragement, I am confident I'll be able to reach the finish line. Basically, I look for any guiltless excuse to carb-load. Please visit my page on the ABTA website to help support my and Maddie's goal. Anything helps, and we greatly appreciate any contributions that you can make.*

*Lastly, I wanted to offer you a few more inspirational words that I have grown to love. I encourage you all to watch former North Carolina State coach Jim Valvano's ESPY speech. His motto for The V Foundation for Cancer Research is "Don't give up, don't ever give up." He ended the speech by stating, "Cancer can take away all my physical abilities; it cannot touch my mind, it cannot touch my heart, and it cannot touch my soul, and those three things are going to carry on forever."*

*What. . . did you think this was meant to be a sentimental letter? Not a chance. I am going to fight through this because that is frankly all I know. And I expect you, too, to fight beside me.*

*All my best,*

*Joe Fulton*

I raised a lot of money with that letter—nearly $20,000. I sent it to every person who wrote me a card, and nearly all of them contributed. Even the three radiation guys donated some money. I hoped that the ABTA would invest that money into clinical research and support for caregivers.

I also sent that letter to my colleagues. Everyone I worked with knew by now. The company had a picture of me wearing two boxing gloves that former colleagues gave me to symbolize me beating the tumor. I was the poster child at work, being the *face* of cancer. Now over seven thousand employees worldwide had seen the picture. I wanted them to focus on the cancer portfolio this company produces. Protect one of your own by laying more of a focus on that. Act with urgency. This was me grandstanding but crying for someone to help me.

Running a mile was so tough. Writing that letter for the ABTA was so easy. I had to practice, but I didn't want to. After procrastinating, I went downstairs from my apartment to the gym to stretch my legs. I lifted my feet and started running.

After running only a mile in my lifetime, in those good ol' high school days, I conquered a 5K. I thank the steroids. They are the best drugs in the world. Anything is possible on steroids. At times they have the worst side effects. But I thank them for giving me that confidence.

As a little warm-up for Chicago, I had to train for a half-marathon in April of 2018. That warm-up became harder as those steroids tapered off quickly. I was screwed for the half-marathon. Not only that but running was so boring to me. It is so monotonous. Not even my "RUN" playlist on Spotify could help. I didn't even factor in the chemotherapy. The thought of this became an added reason as to why I SHOULD attempt this. Face adversity when given the chance.

I would run 5Ks, 10Ks, and eventually ten miles with Maddie. She knew I was too lazy to run by myself, especially outside in the cold. She had already run a couple of marathons in college. She repeatedly told me that her passion started with that classic 26.2 bumper sticker. I can't blame her; my career as a pharmacist came from a career aptitude test during my freshman year of high school.

The race crept up quickly, but I had ammo for the half-marathon. I had stashed leftover steroids from my radiation and pills for my seizures. There was nothing I could do about the chemotherapy, which I had started over a month before. I was running on will and drugs—will in the beginning and drugs at the end.

I ran the race like Mario Kart.

I was competing against other people instead of the race.

Sometimes the same person would catch up to me. I hit the *Bullet* and ran as fast as possible to pass them.

By the tenth mile, I was completely gassed. I was any other pharmacist's worst nightmare. I brought a fanny pack to store my phone and, most importantly, my drugs. My precious drugs. All the uppers and all the downers.

I popped dexamethasone to propel me and lorazepam whenever I felt a seizure coming on. I took a mix of steroids and benzodiazepines to cross the finish line.

After the race, my body just wanted to say "hello" and "goodbye" to our friends who came to support us. I needed a nice nap. My legs were exhausted. For a full marathon, I would think that they'd fall off.

I couldn't run the Chicago Marathon. I couldn't even train for it. My body had been beaten up so much. The fatigue, chemotherapy, seizures, and weight loss are a few factors that had gotten to me. I failed. I had promised a full marathon in my letter and couldn't do it. But someone did it for me. That's how you know that you have an incredible support system holding you up. I had Jaclyn do it without even asking her. She signed up for the race once she had received my letter.

She is my best female friend. We grew up together. We even worked together. I know some of her major milestones in life, even some personal stories we share with each other and no one else. Jaclyn has always been a true friend with no judgment for what we've done or are currently doing.

True unconditional love. They say love comes in pieces that can be broken apart. Though not a romantic love, an almost two-decade relationship is as strong as it ever can be. I may not live twenty years moving forward, but she is a major part of my life. She is a part of *who Joe is.*

Jaclyn had never run a race before, which is mind-boggling. Zero, zip. She did Avon 39 Walks in honor of her aunt who died from breast cancer. Jaclyn held a spin class every day. She was in shape.

She hardly trained for the marathon. I was in Chicago cheering her on, doing my best to support Jaclyn. Sometimes it takes a team to accomplish a mission. When you fall during a race or life, there will be someone that lifts you up. You don't even have to ask. Out of the purity of our hearts, somewhere, love for one another exists.

That girl finished the race on my behalf—the girl who could do anything. Two years ago was the New York City marathon. Finished. Last year was the Philadelphia marathon. Finished. This year, London. All contributions went to the ABTA.

It formed a tradition. She perfected the *ugly cry* when crossing the finish line. Jaclyn dealt with a lot of crap throughout her life. I hope she got some demons out during the process.

It took me years to fully understand this part. It all started with Jaclyn and a lot of deep reflection. When people offer to help, it's a hidden message that THEY genuinely want to help. When others say, "I'm here for anything you may need," give them a piece of something they could help with. When someone offers a home-cooked meal when you can't cook for yourself because of fatigue, let them cook a meal. Pride gets in the way. I was so stubborn to feel as if I could fight this by myself. But I couldn't be Superman anymore, no matter how tough it was. I tried and tried, and if I couldn't do something, I would just tough it out. I'd eventually give up.

I've heard this one hundred times before and consistently declined. It's not for you; it's for THEM. They feel helpless. They feel alone, too. You're not allowing them in. They can't do anything but watch you suffer. So let THEM feel better about themselves. Letting them help you will let them feel better. You must realize this. Stop being so selfish as I was.

I have a friend right now who's going through a tough breakup, and I offered my help. She declined any assistance no matter how much I tried to convince her. Everyone needs help sometimes. Let others in.

## THE NEED FOR SUCCESS

I began my chemotherapy on March 12, 2018. I was back to work by then. I still couldn't speak or articulate. My ambitiousness and wallet forced me to return to work too early. I became sad over not being able to join my team. This was the one thing I had control over, and cancer tried to take it away. I wouldn't let it, even sacrificing my health if necessary. *Just fake it, Joe. Fake the severity of your illness.*

In this situation, I couldn't trust anyone. I didn't want to be let go. Companies put shareholders first and employees second. Even if I were the poster boy, I had to perform in the face of adversity. I had to do this one by myself. So, I had to work, start chemotherapy, and resume school part-time. . . working on my MBA was not necessary, and I did it for reasons I don't understand. It would have made no difference in my career path. But I was addicted to success. My success was defined by what I accomplished. Numerous degrees, awards from the companies I worked at and other organizations, and a bunch of other accolades. Chemotherapy, in addition to work and school, was my next goal.

I had been at my job for less than a year and felt like I had something to prove. I worked my ass off more than anyone will ever understand, staying up all night to read an article that someone else could read and digest in under ten minutes. I barely understood the article. *Fake it, fake it, fake it.*

When I was speaking on calls, I got a "Chill dude" out of Maddie when I hit my desk out of frustration. I couldn't decide when to speak up or not on these calls. It drove me crazy that I wouldn't be surprised if people took pity on me. But I wanted to be seen as a peer and not that *cancer kid.*

I was initially uncomfortable returning to work. I couldn't just say "Thank you." On a team call, everyone spoke and said how much they missed me, and I turned it into a joke. Of all the mistakes I made regarding work, that is right up there with them. Suppose others comfort you or say nice words about you—it's okay to thank them. Direct praise is something I'll always have trouble with. If I could go back, I would be more grateful that they're being honest and vulnerable and not to be insensitive by passing it off as a joke.

My family, friends, colleagues, and even outsiders, thank you.

# CHAPTER 3:

# HORNET'S NEST

Chemotherapy was a lot harder than I ever expected. Half of me wanted to scream and the other half wanted to cry. I was bouncing back and forth between them. There was no in-between. Each dose was a poison I was purposely putting in my body.

I was twenty-eight years old, fit, and strong. I was in ideal shape. I couldn't believe how terrible chemotherapy was. Much more than I thought. Am I just a wuss? Older people were taking the same thing, and here I was, shrugging into a ball. I had a body built to handle these drugs, and I couldn't even tolerate them.

If only I could reach the tumor. . . I would pull the entire thing out of my skull. It was a severe itch I couldn't scratch. That's what chemotherapy felt like to me. It made me handicapped at times. That part was so frustrating.

There was a time when I was taking work calls while receiving an intravenous bag filled to the brim with this toxin. Whenever I attempted to speak, a chill ran down my spine, followed by a gag coming up from my esophagus. But I was still working, still receiving paychecks. No sooner than I left the infusion center, the spewing of everything my stomach contained poured out. If any one of my colleagues had known this, they would have been terrified. If they knew the real story of what happened after these work calls, they might have forced me to return on disability leave. I was very good at downplaying things.

My ambition and stubbornness outweighed the puking and pain.

"Let me have a normal life," I prayed. This time with desperation.

The cancer had to interfere with that, but it couldn't stop me up to that point. . . there was no going back now.

The despair of it all was grim. I wished I could fast-forward to see what life would be like in the future, only if there was a future. I was only one cycle in and I was experiencing worse physical symptoms than just bouts of puke. The chemotherapy was so bad that it gave me a long-lasting gift—peripheral neuropathy. The stinging up and down my right knuckle was unbearable at first. It's been five years, and I can still feel it. There was no UNO Reverse card on this. I learned to deal with it.

There's nothing quite like peripheral neuropathy. The pain won't stop, even if I'm not thinking about it. It is not psychological. It is just pure pain.

Pain during the day.

Pain when I go to sleep.

Pain typing.

Pain throwing a football.

The pain never changes and never stops. I could feel it burning within me—a great reminder of going through chemotherapy.

That drug was stopped immediately. I learned that this was one of the side effects of vincristine that my neuro-oncologist tried to warn me about. I had to protect my body at all costs. My body couldn't risk any more damage than it already had. I don't know why they used that in the three-drug cocktail. Vincristine penetrated the brain less than ninety-nine percent anyway.

As my neuro-oncologist tried to convince me, I was sticking to the plan. Go with PCV. Temodar was not a consideration.

Not much has changed in clinical research about the disease. I imagine the drug company was like "Screw it. It isn't worth the research and development costs."

So, I moved on to the second two drugs of PCV: lomustine and procarbazine. They came as innocent little pills. I don't know what I was expecting. Large, horse-sized pills?

The first few weeks were easy and not what I expected at all. I underestimated them for sure. However, I quickly realized they had packed the power of a monster. A monster that was disturbing.

In weeks four through seven, I was puking nonstop after I took those *innocent* little pills. I'll give you some examples of how untimely they could be:

I threw up for a half hour with only ten minutes to spare before giving an important lecture to my colleagues. There was no time for a quick brush of the teeth. I needed to get my senses back.

I had to press down on my gag reflex, located on the palm, while giving a two-part lecture on cannabinoids. My hand was bright red each time, and it hurt like hell.

I had to enter the restroom to avoid puking in front of one of our major clients. I carried around orange Tic Tacs and ondansetron whenever I was in the field, in addition to my seizure pills. I walked out of there dizzy because of the lorazepam I had taken. I couldn't screw up an important presentation like that one.

I was preparing a seminar given to over two hundred healthcare professionals, all before emptying my stomach multiple times in the company restroom. My team was all gathered around me in the hallway, and they didn't realize why I was frequently running to "pee." As I walked out of the bathroom for the third time, I heard: "Joe Fulton will speak about his amazing journey with cancer. Give him a round of applause!" It would not be a good career move if I threw up on the same stage that the CEO would be standing on directly after my presentation.

## FRAGILITY

Every chemotherapy cycle was a mess. My lymphocyte count and clotting factors would drop so low that the nurse had to call and say, "Be careful; you don't want to accidentally cut yourself. Don't scrape your elbow on something. You're at a risk of bleeding out." I was already anemic.

This conversation happened over and over. Treatment was delayed until my counts returned to the normal range. That was the situation I was facing. This extended the time being on chemotherapy. More nausea, more vomiting, more constipation, more fatigue.

Don't let anyone tell you that being fatigued just means you're tired. There were days I struggled to get up from bed to cook or even grab a glass of water. There were some days I didn't eat at all. Having fatigue feels like there are ten-pound weights all over your body. If you're trying to lose weight, just go on the chemotherapy diet. It really works. According to the scale, I lost forty pounds. Those were pounds I didn't want to lose. I looked fragile. After each cycle, as soon I began to feel better, I would eat the entire cabinet of food in an attempt to put on weight for the next cycle, only to starve again when I was back on treatment.

Never underestimate someone going through chemotherapy. The feeling inside your body is rough. The outside appearance can make anyone self-conscious. Commend anyone who is up and walking while on these dirty drugs.

I noticed clumps of my hair falling out during radiation, months prior. The "Flow" as I called it. . . which nobody else did. I'll never forget how fun it was to shave the Flow off. Maddie and I had exposed the beautiful yet terrifying scar that wrapped along the base of my temporal lobe, to near the top of my head, and snaking back down under my ear. The scar resembled one half of a baseball. I was Uncle Fester in the mirror.

The scar was the first thing people saw when they noticed my face before they could even make their way toward my eyeballs. It was proudly showing itself off. It demonstrated how tough I was and what I had gone through. And kept on going through. Unfortunately, it did not always turn out so well.

I was at a work function with ten neurologists present, showing off my bald head, playing it cool and confident. Make a comment and I won't care. One of the neurologists made a comment, however. He did so in an awkward way. My eyes are down here, buddy.

"What is that?" This guy stared at the scar. He asked in a curious way that brought me down again. My self-esteem collapsed at the speed of light. I was already sick, and the perceived judgment had already made me sicker.

"It's from a brain surgery."

"Oh. Is it cancer?"

"Yes." He's a physician who specializes in neurology. He should know what this obvious incision on my head means. On the other hand, maybe he was just wondering. Maybe he thought it was something different. But still. Work sent me here, and thus I'm here. Doing my job.

He didn't know what kind of an emotional trigger he had set off. In my mind, he was asking, *you're going to die soon.* The scar was a clear sign something wrong had happened to me that I could not hide. I wanted to escape.

I would have to spend the next six months post-radiation for my crusty hair to return. It would be thinner in some spots; I just didn't know where. I hated it most of the time. I liked it sometimes. I had to deal with it all the time.

I ditched my backward snapback hats in public places to see how it felt to be outwardly judged.

I had a friend who was in a dental program while I was in pharmacy school. She had ovarian cancer and suffered from hair loss due to the type of chemotherapy she was on. My friend had a long hiatus from school to grieve and probably handled it worse than I did.

Whenever she went out, she wore a wig, and since I already knew her, I immediately noticed it. This person was shy. She didn't like going out. But when she did, I was so proud of her.

That was her way of showing confidence in the face of cancer. I would always root for her internally when I saw her in person or on social media. I believe it's much harder to lose your hair when you're a female instead of a male. Quite obviously. Selfishly, I wish I had gradually gained that increasing confidence as she did. To know she wouldn't be judged—she owned that. Her courage reminds me of a poem by William Ernest Henley called *Invictus*. It demonstrates power and authority, and I've grown to love it.

*Out of the night that covers me,*

*Black as the pit from pole to pole,*

*I thank whatever gods may be*

*For my unconquerable soul.*

*In the fell clutch of circumstance*

*I have not winced nor cried aloud.*

*Under the bludgeonings of chance*

*My head is bloody, but unbowed.*

*Beyond this place of wrath and tears*

*Looms but the horror of the shade,*

*And yet the menace of the years*

*Finds and shall find me unafraid.*

*It matters not how strait the gate,*

*How charged with punishments the scroll,*

*I am the master of my fate,*

*I am the captain of my soul.*

## WAKE-UP CALL

It was 2:00 a.m. on a Tuesday. I woke up with a bad aura. I climbed out of bed, knowing something was wrong. It was a twitch. I had just begun tapering off steroids. I thought my battles with seizures were over. Not even close. My lip quivered. Then it happened.

I hopped up on my toes while the seizure passed. I couldn't speak when the seizure was occurring. My lips wouldn't purse. Maddie was so confused as to why I was jumping out of bed in the middle of the night. I didn't know if I would ever come out of it. I need some help now! I frantically called the hospital and spoke to the fellow once it had finally stopped.

"Just wait it out. Call the doctor when he gets in," was what the fellow told me. Unfortunately, there was nothing she could do.

I stopped sweating. Finally, I calmed down. I'd be fine. I felt grateful that I didn't pass out in my sleep because my airway may have been blocked. But there was no way I was going back to sleep until I spoke to my epileptologist. I prayed this would never happen again. Not only did I have cancer, but this was an added thing to worry about.

Obviously, I would need a dose adjustment. I need to up my dose on Keppra and I would be fine. Just wait.

"Let's go higher on the Keppra," the epileptologist said when he got in. I was the priority. One can never tell how things will pan out.

And I was fine. . . until the next one came.

Then I started to count.

Then I stopped counting.

The seizures never stopped. Spring was on its way. Every day I wondered when they would stop? Each time it happened, I would shed a tear. Then I remembered I would have to remain tough.

I could survive these, I would survive these, and I would eventually get rid of them. . . I had hoped.

"Let's add another drug," my epileptologist said. Of course, I would have to add another drug; that's what I was thinking the whole time. We had already maxed out the Keppra dosage. I was still seizing every day. Another drug came on board. The seizures didn't lessen.

By April, we added three seizure medications. It became hard to keep count of the total amount of drugs I was taking. With all medications lined up, they took up the ledge of the entire sink. It was a buffet of medicine. A grand total of ten drugs. Oh, and chemotherapy. I added more. Bottle by bottle, swallowing them one by one.

I was having seizures every day, and by the grace of God, no one from work found out. If I was on a call, I used the old "my phone died" tactic. Resetting my phone was a perfect excuse and made sense. I have yet to have a seizure during a live meeting. I may be jinxing myself.

The extra seizure drugs worked, but only for a few days, and then the seizures started again. I couldn't catch a break. I have to deal with headaches, fatigue, chemotherapy, fear of not performing at work (actually hurting the business), and these refractory seizures.

I was wondering how many head hits I could take until I developed chronic traumatic encephalopathy. At this rate, I'd get there before the end of the year. The doctor assured me that wouldn't happen. With the *Fulton luck*, you should never count me out.

In time, he was going to have to switch the third one for a new one. I couldn't take all these drug changes, but what's the other option? Nothing.

Seizures were the primary loss of hope. Never would I be the man I thought I would be. I was just a kid who was ill with a brain tumor. That was one thing I hoped to accept. But these seizures were killing my self-esteem. Every single seizure was like, "Hey, just a reminder, you have cancer." I've had way over a thousand seizures by now. Maybe two thousand or three thousand. I don't even know. All I know is that there must be some miracle drug out there.

Seizures cost me a whole lot more than I could ever imagine. They cost me the quality of life I believe I deserved. From the time I woke up, throughout the day, into the evening, and even when I went to sleep, I was in constant fear of having another one.

They mostly start with an aura; a tingle on my lips or pressure on the neck. The pressure on my neck doesn't go away until I either have a seizure or rest. My other trigger is food. When I don't eat, I'm prone to having them. But being *hungry* is a choice word. Hunger feels like a punch in the pit of the stomach. Such a weird feeling. If I eat, then I'm okay. Every time I go to sleep, I wake up at about 2:00 a.m. or 3:00 a.m., have a snack ready on my side table, munch it in the dark, and take more of my medications, which usually last until lunch. I was living my life carrying snacks around, just in case. I was trying to avoid public places where I may have one.

The fear I live in because of a breakthrough seizure is constant. Nearly paranoid. Although my voice seems to improve after one, it's still not worth it. I don't want to experience a headache . . . or another consecutive seizure! I can't work out, be too hot, or be hungry. Those are my triggers. Every time I have one, it's just plain annoying. But I'm conscious and aware.

At this point, when I have one, I'll just act like nothing even happened.

There are many causes of epilepsy, and I bet some patients would pray to have the same type that I do. If you look on the downside, yeah, it sucks to have refractory epilepsy. On the upside, I should be thankful for the type that I have. I'm sure many mothers and fathers with children would be jealous or envious of my type. They'd be angry that I'm making a big deal out of these. Patients with generalized seizures would take my type over anything. Some patients can't work like I can because of this. I can't ignore reflecting on these blessings.


## ROCKY

I was leading a weeklong medical meeting shortly after returning to work and took on the role against my manager's recommendation. She knew I wasn't ready and was trying to save me from myself. Commenting on health issues is barred from work. Being back at work would have to be cleared by my doctor. There was little she could do. By returning to work with no restrictions, I was expected to do the job I was paid to do.

But I was stupid and stubborn. The *nobody can stop me* attitude was in full effect back then. In hindsight, I shouldn't have even flown to Los Angeles for that conference. My colleagues didn't stay the entire seven days. They stayed maybe for four or five days. But I was the leader, the strongman, holding down the fort for the rest of the group. I stayed for eight days, trying to prove to everyone that I was capable of anything.

I felt good as I arrived at the hotel. It had been a long flight, so I had to relax and fall asleep.

"Oh my God, this bed is so uncomfortable." I woke up in the middle of the night writhing in pain.

I called downstairs. "You have to give me another room. This is the most painful bed I have ever slept in. Jesus Christ."

"Sir, we have no more rooms."

"Well, switch mine with someone else." That was an irrational thought at two in the morning.

"We could call the hospital for you."

"No, no."

The pain only worsened. I ended up sleeping on the floor. It got worse. I did some yoga but the pain wouldn't stop. The right side of my back hurt like a bitch. Something was definitely wrong.

I needed medical attention.

I called back down. Reluctantly, I said, "I need an ambulance."

Crawling on the floor, I finally made it to the elevator. I saw the doorman and yelled for help like a beggar. He helped me up and dragged me to the sidewalk. I face-planted, spending the next ten minutes on the sidewalk screaming for someone to help me. Instead, the hotel employees stared at me trying to figure out what was happening. I just had to lay there curled up in a ball.

The EMT finally arrived to pick me up. This pretty boy walked out all smug, chewing gum, slick haircut, and staring at me like I couldn't handle a little pain. "Help me! Give me morphine." That's how desperate I was. He was in no rush to take me to the hospital. He only tested my vital signs.

Meanwhile, I desperately pleaded with him to put me in the ambulance and drive off. There was no urgency, though. He didn't care and made that totally obvious.

The hospital took forever to process me. I was in a small room facing a random guy standing alongside that twerp with his hands crossed as I was kneeling in pain. They saw me squirm and didn't care. I needed to get in a bed stat.

Room 01. I made it. The pain was worsening as I kept screaming louder and louder. I overheard the nurses at the roundtable saying I was just pill-seeking. It was my first night in Los Angeles, and the hospital had already found me. It seemed that my body could do nothing right. I begged for morphine from the doctor, who had probably seen it all before. From personal experience, I witnessed pill seekers all the time when I was working in a retail pharmacy.

All of the sudden, I heard the nurses taunting me! "Tylenol and Toradol," they said. Loud enough as they passed by my bed. I would've been so pissed if I had time to be pissed. Just a little morphine was all I was asking for. If they could see the tears from pain, they would realize that I'm not a druggie trying to get my hands on oxycodone. Then again, I don't blame them—I looked homeless in my faded shirt, hiked-up shorts, and with only socks on, rocking the bedhead and walking hunched from the discomfort. It wasn't until the CT scan that they found the 8 mm kidney stone.

Now they believed me. By the time 5:00 a.m. rolled around, I finally got the morphine I had been begging for. It was a very, very, very agonizing experience.

A quirky doctor came in that morning, and I was hesitant about him from the start. But what choice did I have? I can't pick and choose doctors in a desperate situation. I was given two options. The first one was extracorporeal shockwave lithotripsy, which involved me missing a few days of the conference.

The second, drink gallons upon gallons of water to pass it. Obviously, I was going to go with the second option, which happened to be the most painful. It would take fluids, running in place, and facing pain that even the strongest of drugs couldn't stop.

I don't know how many gallons I drank or hours I spent running in place, but I do remember that bloody stone coming out. No matter what, the conference must go on. My kidneys were sore and I was peeing blood for a couple of days. I would refuse my manager's plea to rest and relax. I needed to lead this conference. Even a kidney stone couldn't stop me.

My epileptologist said I was the one percent who developed kidney stones on that medication—*Fulton luck*. Not only was I still having seizures, but I also had to change medications again during this conference. I was disappointed that it wasn't a natural kidney stone but a medication-induced one. Cross that drug off the list. On to the next medication.

He had me switch to another seizure drug that needed to be monitored. But I'd have to get the levels checked when I got back. I can still remember the smell of those large pink pills from the new drug. What I don't remember was everything else at that conference. I vaguely remember seeing Slash in LAX; I just don't remember the flight back, the Uber home, or the lapses of time in between. That damn new drug caused amnesia.

But one thing I remember was seizing out multiple times with Maddie present. She was shoving more benzodiazepines down my throat. She took it upon herself to treat me.

I can't confirm if the rest of these are true. Maddie said she had to hold me up to bathe. She remembered us going out and me drooling uncontrollably. She made fun of the situation. I had no memory of this. She knew something was wrong. Maddie figured that since I had a checkup appointment in two weeks, she would just wait it out.

The time came to attend my doctor's appointment. When she brought me to the doctor's office, I couldn't even stand. My eyes rolled around. I fell off the chair.

Afterward, I thought, how was this not a red flag for you? She had the knowledge to recognize what valproate toxicity looks like. She's a pharmacist!

I finally woke up in the hospital two days later having no clue what happened. Apparently, I never got my drug levels checked after all until I was under inpatient care. My epileptologist dropped the ball to get them checked once I got back from Los Angeles. The tingling I felt on my body wouldn't cease until the fourth day. It was honestly torturous.

Developing carpal tunnel syndrome was the icing on the cake.

With a foggy brain, I called my manager and cried that I let the team down. I was trying to do something and failed at it. I wanted to prove to myself that I could handle anything. The rest of my colleagues were worried. They were worried about my health. I worried that I kept letting people down.

I was disappointed for a couple of reasons. One, I hated the hospital and wished I had never gone back. Second, Maddie and I were supposed to leave for Greece the next day. I had put that on my to-do list. My body was betraying me. I felt like a rag doll being poked and prodded by needles, hooked up to machines, listening to endless beeping sounds. There was nothing I could do about the Greece trip. I was helpless.

"I got our tickets refunded. You don't know what I went through to cancel them," said Maddie with an unforgiving tone in her voice.

Clearly, she was frustrated. But what could I do? I was strapped to a hospital bed that I couldn't get up from. An alarm would go off if I tried. I wanted to get out of the hospital even more than she did. She even spent her nights at home. She was much different than she had been after the surgery. Her anger about what happened shone through. But weaning off this toxic drug and switching onto another medication before I could leave was necessary. There were five more days to go. I was held captive by emotions this time—just sitting there, waiting for valproate to exit completely, and angry as hell at my body for failing me repeatedly.

On the last day, Maddie brought in a social worker. This lovely woman came in with her as a sort of mediator. To be honest, I don't know why she was there at all. It was clear she was uncomfortable. My thought was that Maddie wanted a free couple's therapy session. That poor woman had no training in this. Maddie just found and forced anyone who would listen into my hospital room. We just sat in silence at first.

Uncomfortably, I broke the ice.

"It's not like I want to be in this bed." Utter silence. "Do you think I chose to have a brain tumor?"

"It's been really hard for me." This was the first time in two and a half years that I saw Maddie tearing up. I didn't think it was humanly possible for her to show emotion.

This was the beginning of the end.

She broke up with me a short time after. The cancer had finally ruined my hopes and dreams. It killed me more than I could put into words. My girlfriend. . . correction, ex-girlfriend. . . was the last thing a brain tumor could take away.

Thinking back to when I laughed at this brain tumor when calling my friends, to Maddie breaking up with me, having lost everything I had, was the perfect setup. I thank God for my friends because I don't know how I could do it otherwise.

I gave her an out.

She could have ended this relationship before my surgery, and it would feel a lot better than her giving up on us after just five months. I would rather miss having Maddie around than her breaking up with me like that. Maddie never faced real adversity before, so she gives up when a thing like this happens. Maddie didn't want to be the primary caregiver, and that's totally okay. The problem was her committing to that role in the first place. I should have had someone else, like a family member of mine, to take on that role.

I was going to marry this girl.

There's something to be said about a person being in a long-term relationship and giving up on it five months into a diagnosis. We had never fought at all before this. So that answers the question. It wasn't "in sickness and in health." The breakup was so sudden. *Let me recover from that hospital visit first.*

The saddest part about it is that she didn't do it face-to-face, even though we lived together. She officially ended it while I was recovering at my sister's. *Okay, well, I'll see you in two days.*

I had an uncomfortable couch to look forward to when I got back. The obvious worn-in couch embraced me as I sunk in. Our pictures, our marathon medals, and *our* bed were taunting me. Dreadful to say the least. We were no more than thirty feet apart at any moment because our apartment was so small. Then I got an upgrade to a mattress that lay plopped on the floor in our second bedroom. A little more depressing. This was my permanent bed until we figured things out. And I never entered my former bedroom again.

That replacement bed was actually perfect for my back, but it was bad for my mindset. I slept on that bed for another four months. The idea of facing her every morning, afternoon, and night tormented me. After months of trying to break free of the lease, there was no easy way to get out. I had signed the lease in my name. I was committed to a yearly contract. That two-bedroom corner apartment cost over $2,700 per month, and there was no way I could pay that off. We used to split the cost of rent. But she forced me to front it. I was screwed. I see hell when envisioning that apartment. My own hell was carved out.

The torment became normal for me. I would just hang out in my new room/the office the whole day and do work. I had a little distraction. I focused on my MBA more.

For TV, we'd sit on opposite chairs. For meals, we'd be civil and share. It was confusing because we were broken up and bickered like toxic roommates. The time I spent living there messed me up. I was still dealing with these triple-therapy regimens for seizures in addition to my lorazepam and going for speech therapy a couple of times per week. Oh, and chemotherapy. What a time to be trapped in a breakup.

A complete recovery was impossible, and the stress of living with Maddie only made it worse. I would cry for her to take me back like I was some desperate dog.

That was the lowest I've ever been. Breaking up with someone was not a problem for me, but I quickly learned how demoralizing they can be when you're the person that's being broken up with. Mine was probably worse, knowing I was going through all these factors at the same time.

Eventually, the lease ended and another room opened up. The departure was with mixed emotions. I didn't have Maddie to rely on anymore. What if something seriously bad happened? That fear was shot into sadness when I found out the apartment was on the same floor. Two minutes walking from my door to hers.

The new place was a studio apartment with barely four hundred square feet. It wrapped around the kitchen with only one sliding door. The bed fit in just right. If one needed to use the bathroom, they would have to squeeze between the bed and the drawers to get there. The sink was outside the bathroom, leaving only several footsteps to the door. The kitchen, dining room table, and living room were morphed into one. I worked from the couch. On the walls were a mounted TV, a Banksy picture, and some yellow abstract art picture that I still can't make out.

In addition, my windows looked out into a parking lot that would later become a construction site. Those quarters made it so much more depressing. Being in that place could drive one mad. Switching from 4001 living with her to 4059 alone—it surely brings back PTSD.

*But I was still excited when Maddie would text to come study with her.*

*If I do that, will she get back with me?*

*She'd invite me to her apartment to watch a movie. Will she make a move?*

*She's inviting me to work out with her in the gym. Okay, she's definitely getting back with me now.*

This charade went on for two whole years. Maddie knew what she was doing. She was trying to convince herself. I tried to deny it was guilt, but it was—guilt for having broken up with her boyfriend when he needed her most. Whenever we were in public with our mutual friends, she acted like she didn't know me. She would be okay with acknowledging me when no one else was around. Maddie was embarrassed. She called me her friend. I was always her ex-boyfriend. Dangling me by a string was the only way she could rest peacefully at night. She didn't want to lose me, but at the same time, she didn't want me.

I received a lot of flak from my friends about the way she was messing with my mind. Every one of them would get angry on my behalf after that.

"Why the hell would you see her? She's playing games with you. She's just getting in your head." I heard the same thing from everybody. But love is a wild thing.

I still loved her in some messed up way.

Sometimes my friends got aggressive when speaking about her. I would always defend her to this day. "She's good, just not the right one for me." I secretly agreed with my friends but refused to talk negatively about her. It was bad Karma, and I needed all the Karma I could get.

I spoke to her sister about a year and a half after we split to figure out where I stood in relation to Maddie. And I'm still good friends with her sister to this day.

I asked her, "Will I ever be a part of your family?" She gave me the bluntest answer that I ever received—a simple "No." Well, I needed to hear that.

Sometimes I need a dose of reality to hit me square in the face. A lot of people have told me that I have a thick skull. I couldn't let this seep into my heart. I was beginning to see the manipulative side of Maddie's sweet face. I also think and know that her family influenced her not to return to the *cancer boy*. And I can't put the blame fully on her, but what I do blame is the way she went about it.

At the time, I was too weak with all I was going through, both physically and mentally. I could barely make it out of bed in the morning. With Maddie, it was my fault for wanting a little company and human interaction. I was sad and borderline depressed. My fatigue didn't give my body enough energy to be fully depressed. Plus, I had to survive to beat this tumor. I needed to get my seizures under control, undergo this rough chemotherapy, and finish my MBA that I'd been working on for years. That was going to be my focus, my cross to bear. I was going through it alone. I thought if I asked Maddie for help, she would see how sick I actually was and instill in her that she did the right thing.

## TEARS IN HEAVEN

My friends stepped up and were there for me. Even though I could only stay up until 8:00 p.m., that's all I needed. It was beautiful to see the compassion my friends showed. I only remember them as dumb idiots in high school and college. I had not seen this side of them before.

I couldn't drink the first year, so Mike and Matt would come over to play games on the Switch with me. As time passed, if I was down to drink a little, I would, as long as I didn't have an aura. Sometimes I would take benzodiazepines to shrug off the aura. I'd double up on medications occasionally to prevent one from happening. Then there were times I needed someone around if I was self-conscious about my speech. When I could speak logical sentences, my friends would listen in and give me their full attention.

The later it got, the less I could make sense of things.

The crappy part about being my age was when I was invited to a wedding. That seemed to happen every other weekend. Slowly my friends were getting married and starting families. They had competing priorities. I was delighted for them, but envious. They had the life I saw for myself.

My closest friends and I from the post-doctoral fellowship went to a winery in Virginia to celebrate some birthdays, as we frequently did (well, several wineries). On our second stop, my already drunk friend comes up to me and yells:

"Fulton, come over here! I want to talk to you, buddy." I could see the drunk in his eyes and the red wine in his hand. I wanted to know what the big secret was that he would tell me.

"What's up, man?"

"I just wanted you to know that we're all rooting for you."

"What're you talking about? I know you're not rooting against me." That's when the emotions came rising to the top.

"I just want you to know that."

He wasn't letting go of my arm. He was embarrassing me—just like the seizures, adding one more reminder that I will succumb to my brain tumor. I don't think he realized what he was saying. I knew he meant well, but those words should have stayed inside his head.

"I have to use the bathroom. I really have to pee." This was an escape tactic I usually use for Irish Goodbyes. But this time, I was at a random winery in Virginia.

I wonder if he was thinking about that the whole ride down. He was always a funny dude, and then he got so serious at that moment. It didn't matter. Once I reached the bathroom, I bawled my eyes out. All my friends are having fun, and I'm the one who has this tumor in my brain. They all had futures.

This was the most embarrassing moment I'd felt in a long time. I couldn't stop crying. The rest of the day was a nightmare, and the clock wouldn't tick fast enough until we returned to the Airbnb. I didn't want to play card or pong games after that. But I had to join in to not make it look more pitiful if I wasn't there. It goes without saying that I had no fun on that trip. I wish I hadn't gone in the first place. I just wanted to leave Virginia.

When I finally left, I was completely conflicted. Does celebrating the birthdays of Xavier and Lisa outweigh the risk of embarrassment? Twelve of my best friends were there. But I couldn't speak, or smile, or offer anything of substance to the group. I was a useless body. I had to be there, though. These were my friends, and I couldn't break out of the bubble I was in. I learned a lot about myself that day—never hang out with a large group of people like I used to be able to do.

# CHAPTER 4:

# CURSES

My diagnosis can be considered a curse that I deserved. I had been facing harsher realities of life ever since this illness struck me, but some of the things I was told were really jarring. My ex-girlfriend's mom told me I must have done something terrible in my former life. This has stuck with me. I still hear the echo in her voice from time to time. The weight of her words lay heavy. If reincarnation does exist, was I really a bad person. . . like a bank robber, gang member, or maybe something even worse than that? Before this life, what have I done that could've caused such a serious illness? All this negative energy must have swung back around.

Nevertheless, raised Catholic, my beliefs are different. "I believe in the forgiveness of sins." Sister Dorothy, a nun from middle school, drilled that sentence into my classmates' brains. That, I remember! We'd have to say that line every day before class. I still recite that whenever I go to church. These are not necessarily words to live by. Prayers must come from your heart. Sometimes I had a bone to pick with Him—maybe before the diagnosis, maybe after the diagnosis. Nonetheless, we had a rocky relationship.

Do you believe God has a plan for everything, and we just don't know what it means? I seldom lost faith in the beginning. Over time, though, I started to overthink things happening in my life and seemed to question my faith. Of course I sinned. Everyone sins.

But is that what this diagnosis is all about? Is there an underlying message? Maybe I sinned too much—or tumors happen naturally and I'm just unlucky.

Think about anyone who has succumbed to cancer. Then think of how good of a person they were. It always seems to happen that way. I don't really know if I'm a good person or not but I try to be. People tell me I am. Others say, "You do not deserve this."

My mom used to tell me whenever one of my dogs passed away, "God didn't want to wait around. He wanted to bring them up to be with Him sooner." This explanation made sense to me. I'll remind myself of this throughout the day, only to make myself feel better. God wants me with Him.

Do you believe in that?

I always keep in mind that everyone deals with their own crap. Who doesn't have something going wrong in their lives? Everyone carries baggage, whether it be bad or indifferent. Everyone has a story to tell.

My sister is ten years older than me. We grew up with a single mom and two different dads, and we're total opposites. She was always the troubled child, and I was the angel who caused no problems. I never got scolded by my teachers, and she got the *spanking spoon* at home. She's more social, and I don't come close. She looks like her dad, and I am a spitting image of my mom.

As adults, Sydney took a different path. She went to community college, and I went to a prestigious university. She doesn't have a doctorate, and I do. She has the responsibility of taking care of a family, and I don't.

And that's okay. We're two different people bound by my mother's blood. She's got way more stress taking care of other people—her family. My stress is taking care of a dog. But we're close as can be. She has her life. I have mine. That is just family. Our love is, without a doubt, unconditional. The one thing we'll always have in common is a great support system. We love them, and they love us. What could be better than that?

My family has been everything to me lately because only a few of us are left. My mother, father, and sister live in three different states. That's it. I've been adopted into my other friends' families, though. I used to work all through college and pharmacy school, especially the summers, knowing I didn't have much to go back to.

I hate holidays. I'd even work on Christmas and Easter every year. The idea of a big family makes me uncomfortable. Having my friends and colleagues invite me over triggers a bit of social anxiety.

James was my good friend from college. One year, his mother cooked Thanksgiving dinner, packaged it up, and sent it to me. That's an example of how they were: just sweet families matched with good sons. To this day, I'm still uncomfortable in large groups. I hate it. Anxiety and embarrassment from the tumor, I guess.

Even though I'm shy compared to my sister, I used to force myself to be somewhat social. In the past, I attended everything someone invited me to. But that socialite in me has been flipped to the side by my illness, my speech, and the effects of COVID-19—especially the quarantine. I don't think that I or anyone has fully recovered from that.

Now I stay away from big crowds unless my close friends are there with me. I go to random parties or social events with people only if I feel safe. When I know some people that I either don't like or have past relationships with are going, I simply won't go. "I can't come" and then creating an excuse has become the norm.

It's a different kind of life I've gotten used to by now.

Depressing, right? The anxiety and the fact that my life didn't go as planned had turned me into a person on the brink. Everything that happened to me since my diagnosis has made it nearly impossible to get through the day. I somehow do it with a smile on my face. I spare people the feeling burning up inside my chest, just knowing that I'm probably going to die younger than expected, much younger than them. I'm just putting on a front for others.

I am living in a hell that I can't get out of.

But aren't I supposed to live in glorious bliss? With sins, there became consequences. Instead, I must accept that this is my new life. In a way, the tumor is literally part of me. In the making of Joe, there is organic matter, inorganic matter, and a big, fat tumor that makes itself known.

## ACCEPTANCE

We gladly accept the good things in life but we are expected to mutually accept the bad things. The Serenity Prayer says it perfectly. I have to accept the tumor—I don't have to like it, but I must understand that I can't change it. This realization of acceptance has gotten me through this diagnosis. I don't follow it sometimes, but I keep reminding myself about it. The only way we can move on is to accept that fact and everything that comes with it. I'll try my entire life to get there. I will succeed and fail along the way.

The catalyst was the breakup. I was distraught without Maddie. The companionship and support I needed were no longer there. So, my father stepped in when Maddie backed out.

I don't think Maddie ever saw it from my side. When I went into the gym of my apartment building, I was in clear view of her apartment. It was in my face the whole time. I could see if she was away or at home. Whenever the lights were on, my jealous self would peek to see if someone else was there.

Maybe it was her study buddy as she was also pursuing her MBA. Or maybe her friends. Or perhaps it was just family; they came over a lot. The last time I was jealous over a girl was in high school. But this was way different. And the illness made me feel very unwanted.

Darkness fills the room when I look back on it. My memories of that time are covered over in gray clouds that won't go away. When I was *allowed* into her apartment, ninety percent of the time, we'd make popcorn and watch a movie. Or when she was studying, she would let me sit at her table.

How stupid was I?

If it was a clean break, that would be easier than the mind games she was playing with me. It made me want to move out of the building completely.

I'd had four serious relationships in my life up until the diagnosis. Serious enough to not call them flings. There have only been two people I've actually loved. Maddie was one of them. Besides that, you could say I'm a serial dater who only needs comfort. My sister always tells me that. But Maddie was different.

Over time, the chase put me over the top. I couldn't have her back because I was a *cancer boy*, which made it impossible to be loved again.

## STUCK

I had to finish my lease and would buy a home after. But I couldn't go to see homes to buy because of chemotherapy. Realistically, this couldn't happen anyway, as I had to be close to my cancer center. I needed public transportation since I couldn't drive. I was purely stuck in an unhealthy situation. So, I signed up for another year. I had to accept the hours of hope and rejection from Maddie.

Close friends were all I had. Distraction was what I needed. I couldn't do anything physical besides that race because I feared having another seizure. I took nothing of Maddie's when I moved out of the shared apartment—no pictures, nothing sentimental about us. I trashed everything that brought up memories, even that damn medal. I did the race for her and was beside her as we crossed the finish line. I left it. I stuck her with two of the same half-marathon medals.

It cost me $2,300 per month to live in that studio apartment. Every day I was tasked to put on a smile for work. I'd just fake it all. All I needed to do was pretend like everything was normal, but it wasn't. My health routine and all the tests I get has not changed to this day. However, the bloodwork has decreased to once a month.

I was claustrophobic when it came to MRIs at first, and now, I look forward to them. Seizure medications make me sleepy, so the MRI turns into naptime after a two-hour ride to the center. The eight inches in front of me doesn't seem that scary anymore. When I get woken up after fifty minutes, I get really disappointed. Never interrupt a good nap.

This situation was the opposite of when I first started getting MRIs. During the time when Maddie and I were still together, I was getting used to the drill, knowing what to expect. My life has come to this now: outpatient MRIs. My second MRI was a complete mess. It's terrifying in the beginning. The technicians gave me a stress ball. It signals to them that I'm having a problem in the MRI tube.

Early on, I had a seizure before the MRI time was up and was squeezing the ball as hard as I could. About five hospital staff members came running in to see what was happening. They took off my mask immediately. A few of them went into the waiting room and called for Maddie. They probably were calling to let her know I had a seizure; except she wasn't there.

"Maddie. Is she here? Maddie?" one of the technicians called out.

I held onto one of the women's hands, not because of the seizure, but because I had yet to get past the acceptance of the tumor.

Maddie had gone shopping, designer bags and all. Zara. Tiffany. Dior. She never came back to one of my MRIs after that out of pure embarrassment on her part, and mine.

I remember one of the technicians saying, "She should have been here for your support." Maddie was worried about the "mother hens" coming out if she came back to another of my MRIs. So, I used public transportation to my scans.

I didn't realize until after we broke up, but that is the type of girl she was.

## FOUR WALLS

After settling into my new normal, it became apparent that I would spend my whole life like this. Imagine going from the ideal life I had created to complete torture—not just the sadness over Maddie, but the tears of everything that happened. During the first two years in that apartment building, I would cry every day without fail. When I cried, I tried to keep it solely in the shower. I would sit on the floor and let the steamy water wash over my head. There wasn't a day I missed. Maybe I didn't need to shower that day, but I did it anyway, hunched in a ball with my arms crossed.

The water was loud so no one could hear me weep. Yes, I'm talking about my next-door neighbors. They could hear me sobbing anywhere else. Oftentimes, when I was feeling overwhelmed, I took a thirty-minute shower to let all the tears out. It was calming to me, a much-needed ritual in the morning before I'd start the day. Why me? Why me? Game time. I washed my face and that was it. My eyes were sore, but there were no tears left.

I was envious of everyone close to me, although they were all my good friends. But because of social media, it seemed like everyone I knew was out in the world living a life that this brain tumor prevented me from enjoying. I went from self-pity to increasing frustration throughout the day.

First, it was about life, then about work, and eventually, the stress of schoolwork. And then tears started again the next day.

I watched a panel interview on television with some teens that were present during the Parkland shooting. It hit me hard. When a person deals with something death-related, it's sad to come to the realization that there's no coming back from the tragedy that happened. I can never relate to that feeling. I don't understand what it's like to lose a classmate, a friend, or someone you share your deepest secrets with. The trauma these young teenagers must face is awful and so senseless. With our different experiences and paths, these youths and I share one thing in common: tears.

Each of us cried in the shower every single day. It's one of the ways we grieve. That enclosure offers protection—it's a little box shut off from the world. You can sing, hum, and stay as long as you like. The water keeps falling on your face. It's human emotion. We let it all flow out.

"Never let them see you sweat," my grandmother used to tell me. Her energy was so strong that I felt it in me.

I tried to keep all my tears inside the shower as best as I could. I tried to be fierce all along. Crying in front of friends are one thing, but colleagues are another. I tried to leave my personal life out of it, but it always came back to haunt me.

Sometimes I still get the "Are you okay?" Or the "How are you feeling?"

I realize that's a polite thing to do. But I didn't want these people to ask me this question more than once. After a while, I got fed up with the same people wondering how I was doing. My answer wouldn't change.

"Yes. Perfect." I don't know how many times I've answered that question.

My colleagues should get used to respecting my boundaries undoubtedly about my health. The front I put on was how I wanted to be treated.

At one point, I remember being a jerk to a colleague so that they would focus on the words and not the person they were speaking to. I was so self-conscious. That's how much it hurt me. I was unprofessional at work because my feelings overpowered me so much.

Another time a man from a different department had it out for me. He was an ass and I didn't like him from the moment I met him, just because he was rude. I had to remain professional at work no matter the situation, and it didn't matter if I was right or wrong. But I didn't follow this rule. Instead of taking the high road, I took the low road. I wasn't a sucker. I let my feelings of anger come out. He was a jerk, so I was too. I wasn't worried about repercussions. I think I even cursed. The here and now was all that mattered. He started it, and I finished it. I released some anger.

I tried as hard as I could to remain professional. But he kept escalating the situation. Then I realized he wasn't even worth another second of my time.

This random guy who I'd never work with again wasn't worth it. It was a situation where I stood up for myself in the completely wrong way. I don't recommend that to anyone. He was just an easy target. He caught me in a moment where nobody was safe from my attitude. Truthfully, it wasn't him; it was entirely me.

## DISCRIMINATON

My knee hurt so much that I was limping around like my leg was broken. My training for the full marathon (in which Jaclyn ran for me) left me with a runner's knee. I couldn't let it get any worse. Pushing myself on the treadmill was the worst thing I could've done. I had to take care of it immediately and not just wait for it to get worse. I learned my lesson the last time I had waited. . . it delayed the diagnosis of the tumor.

Luckily, I had the best physical therapy center to heal my knee. It was right in my own backyard. Perfect. I'd be on my feet and knee in no time. This was a moment of self-recovery for me. To be concerned about anything else, other than cancer, was helpful for my sanity.

I was genuinely excited to make an appointment for something that had nothing to do with my brain for once. A sense of relief came over me. I had a normal medical appointment—that was huge. It's crazy to be excited about an injury, but in return, it would mask the pain from all the chaos inside of me. The appointment was made as soon as I could reach the phone.

A week later, I was going into the rehabilitation center. It was one of the best in the country. I gladly took the patient information documents from the secretary at the desk. The form was about six pages. Name. . . age. . . medications. . . past medical history. . . I wanted to make sure all of the medical information was accurate and up to date. I didn't have any doctor's appointments at that moment in time. I didn't even have a primary care physician, which was stupid in hindsight.

This was the very first time that I had to check off the "cancer" box at a facility that wasn't affiliated with my cancer center. I was nervous that I'd be perceived differently. But it was my actual diagnosis. I was transparent about it. My surgery had already happened many months ago.

Something seemed fishy as soon as I handed the clipboard back over to the secretary. Then the three staff members sitting behind the counter were chatting behind the desk, but in a whisper, so I couldn't listen in. The one who gave me the clipboard called me up.

"What kind of cancer do you have?"

"Why does it matter? I'm here for my knee. I screwed it up while I was running."

"I'll have to call the director to come down."

"Wait, what? I already said the pain was in my knee."

The knee has no relation to the brain. . . obviously. I selected that damn "cancer" checkmark. I would have no issue here if I didn't check that box. Just fix my knee. I promise brain cancer is not contagious. It was not necessary to have someone come down to meet me. My blood began boiling.

A large man with a straight face came down. "Hi, Joseph. Let me take you to a private room where we can talk."

I couldn't believe what was going on. As we walked through the narrow hallway, I was mentally preparing for how I would respond. I was going to act completely respectful. We sat down. He started.

"We think what's best for you is to go to another facility. There is one right up the street. We can refer you to them."

He was serious. If you just refer me, I'll be back having the same conversation with a different guy there. I wasn't going to comply. This was the best center for rehabilitation. That was the place where I would receive care for my knee.

It was my turn.

"I think you're being a dick right now. You will fix my knee here."

His eyes were wide. He had thought I would just sit down and accept his recommendation. All was quiet. I walked out first. Then he followed.

I was furious. The director went over to the desk, talked to the office staff, and had me scheduled. I'm sure I was the gossip of their facility that day. I didn't care. That's when I realized how cancer could be viewed.

It sucks when you must hide it—not from colleagues, not from friends. The judgment came from strangers. I had to hide my health. If I were to check the "diabetes" box, they would accept me and maybe work around the condition. Say I checked "previous heart condition." They probably would've taken me depending on the time of the event. The rehabilitation center was directly attached to a hospital anyway in case of a medical emergency.

It's safe to say I would never check that box ever again. Not at the dentist, not at urgent care, not at the pharmacy, not on a waiver at the amusement park. Never again. From that point onward, that box went unchecked.

## OPPOSITES

I had the loveliest manager. She would go to bat for me. She was always there if I needed anything. It's not often you have a manager you have the utmost respect for who you can also call a lifelong friend. She would check on me throughout my diagnosis when I was out on disability. She was supportive. When I called her, she always answered. I've learned not to get into specific details when I was on medical disability, but the entire situation was different.

There was a regular-sized pool table downstairs in the apartment building. I remember the chat we had about the Philadelphia Eagles, where the best places to eat were, and the difference in windchill from my area to hers. I struggled with my voice. But she would still listen and laugh.

Inviting me over for dinner was a touching gesture that I gladly accepted. It was just friendly conversation and absolutely no work talk. Having a meal with her family totally felt like visiting a friend and not exactly a manager. I respected her even more. We had a beer on her porch afterward. She no longer works at my company, but I would still go to her when I needed advice.

My current boss is the complete opposite—a selfish person with only his interests in mind. He was a narcissist, too. He and I have a history that goes back over six years. Of course, he was ambitious—nothing wrong with that! But he was too ambitious. He cut down everyone to reach the top. As a person, he was trying to be the cool kid. He had a story for everything. In my mind, I was thinking: This is work. Nobody's impressed. Stop. It's not part of our job description. Realizing he might be my manager potentially for the rest of my career at this company was a nightmare. I loved my job before my previous manager switched.

He was the only one I've ever clashed with at work. When a manager actively prevents you from getting a promotion and a huge raise, it becomes personal. He held grudges like that. So, it didn't surprise me that he would do something inappropriate. Needless to say, I have no respect for him.

The second week he became a manager, out of nowhere, he said, "You can go back on medical leave if you need to."

No examples of anything work-related. Nothing to do with anything I had done. It just came out of nowhere. It blindsided me.

I struggled with my speech at the time, but people knew what I said. If anyone complained, I could see that being a reasonable issue. But he had to come up with specific examples, which he couldn't. He didn't know my clients, nor would he ever. It was a power trip, when I was the one dealing with a brain tumor. I would never stoop so low.

Naturally, I went to Human Resources and told them.

"Just don't let him bring up my health in any work setting," I asked them.

That was my new manager's way of making others uncomfortable in the workplace. Shame on him for trying to use my diagnosis against me. I wasn't astonished, but I was really ticked off. To my surprise, Human Resources did nothing.

A month later, he did the same thing. "If at any point you struggle, feel free to go back on medical leave." No examples. No complaints.

I reported it to Human Resources again. Nothing came of it. They didn't want any problems to occur at the company. I couldn't even trust the people who were there to protect me. Yet, they told the head honcho, and that person didn't do anything about it. My so-called protection was violated. Again.

Four years later, I was stricken with pneumonia. I missed four days, so it didn't count as short-term disability. He changed it to five days so it would. Then, he took away four more vacation days the next week, even though I was still working. It was a clear sign that he still wanted me off his team. He was trying to make the case to his director that "Joe's always sick." It took me three months and a lot of stress to get that claim overturned. Two other people had a sickness during the same period and didn't have the same experience that I did. It was such a petty thing to do. I had nobody in my corner. But I had the doctor's note. Even the doctor thought it was a joke.

Let's set up a scenario. For instance, if I were to say, "I can't do my job the way it's supposed to be done because of my tumor," I could talk about options with my manager. There's a very thin line when you mention the possibility of going on leave. But at no point should you force someone to go on leave unless they're underperforming.

Even so, bringing it up is inappropriate and morally wrong. That's why "we don't discriminate against anyone because of a disability" is written on every corporate job description. This was my manager on an ego trip and on his way to Human Resources violations quicker than I thought.

Karma's a bitch, as he eventually did.

How could I feel comfortable at work anymore if my diagnosis will just be used against me? Nothing was going my way. My sense of normalcy was utterly absent in the workplace.

Remember to put on a smile. Be professional. In other words, be fake Joe. I was determined not to give the tumor the satisfaction of killing me. Even if I was the poster boy of inspiration for some or the pity boy who's sick for others, at least I kept going. It felt like I was holding up a boulder. And maybe I was.

My grandmother was right. "Never let them see you sweat." Otherwise, they will take advantage of you.

## STRUGGLES

Radiation is one of the things that still affects me. New people I meet don't notice it, but I'm not as sharp as I once was. When I pause mid-sentence to gather my thoughts, it still makes me frustrated. I can't think as quickly to answer a question.

I have moments where I want to start over at a new company. When applying for new jobs, I give the greatest presentation, but when it comes to the Q&A section, I always fail. Similarly, the same things happen while talking with friends. I pause for a while to gather my thoughts. That's how I know the effects of radiation are separate from anxiety or stress.

Optimism is one of the things that I try to bring every single day at work. It works in most cases.

On the first call with my previous manager, she said, "You should put your focus on these three things":

1. Family and friends.
2. Your health.
3. Work.

A work-life balance. That's what matters. Although work affects both my mental and physical state, I will work for as long as I can. *Fake it until you make it.*

## DREAD OF NEW RELATIONSHIPS

I had to get over Maddie before I could ever date again. I couldn't bring feelings for someone else into a brand-new relationship. At least, that's my perspective. I wanted to get over her first. Completely over her. Others handle it differently, but that's my view on serious relationships now. But first, I needed to recover from chemotherapy. That would set me back a year. Then I had to wait a while for my flow to grow back to cover up my scar. That would take a long time because the radiation was making it grow back slower and crunchier. I figured recovery from seizures was a lost cause.

All in all, about two years seemed like a realistic timeline.

First of all, dating is the worst, especially in your thirties. All these apps encourage a person to try on as many people as possible for size and then decide whom they like the best. It was a competition over the hottest girl, and then the non-attractive ones were pushed to the side. The same goes for us men—it's a battle to be the most handsome and successful guy. I was not too fond of that. People were getting serious about dating and wanting to settle down. I don't have time for lunch or dinner dates. Or the hiking dates. Everything is exhausting when it comes to finding love.

My previous girlfriends all started out as friends. But I had to find some sort of companionship to restore my self-esteem. I was lonely—lonely sleeping by myself, lonely cooking for myself. I barely had any single friends left anymore. They were all taken. Unfortunately, my times of being social, where I would meet new people, were not possible because of my illness.

Using these dating apps gave me no hope at all. My self-esteem was already at rock bottom; any sort of rejection would push me over the edge. I'd swipe, being extremely picky with my selections. I matched with some good-looking girls. Messaging them wasn't the problem. I could make any woman swoon with my texting skills. They were top-notch. But meeting women face-to-face was the harder part. I didn't socially interact with many people at that point and now I have to buy some girl food to impress her. So much work!

I was still brain-damaged at this point, now and forever. This time I had to be the pursuant. The first girl I met, Laura, wanted to go on another date. I told her straight up that there wasn't a connection.

It was mainly pride that held me back.

At first, I figured dating would always be like this.

I was so relieved that someone wanted me, that they were interested—that they could see everything on the surface was normal besides my speech and hair. Somehow, Laura looked past that.

The second date was the exact opposite. She kept me waiting in the bar until she was able to get out of work. That's what hard-working professionals do. I love that ambition. She looked beautiful in her work clothes. I would be okay with dating her. The problem is that I was too confident coming off the last date. This time my date did not end well.

I called my friend Owen after to fill him in.

"It was more like an interview. You would have found it hilarious if you were a fly on the wall." I told him how awkward it was.

"It was a back-and-forth the whole time. She went to Notre Dame. Her parents all went to Notre Dame. And I spent the entire time making fun of their football team. She did NOT like it." Owen kept laughing. I was going for playful banter. I may have offended her—well, definitely. What I did was inappropriate. But Notre Dame football does suck.

"She even left her beanie there." I was laughing as well.

Online dating is in fact an interview. The typical relationships I've been in just happen naturally. They happen when I don't try. With online dating, I must learn how to date again without saying off-putting things. I have remembered that a date is a first impression. Essentially, I couldn't be my *real* self. My *real* self is awkward. I'm too blunt.

I had to stray outside of who I naturally was. I had to put on this persona of what my dates expected. I just acted like I was going to dinner with a friend. But they were not my friends. They were strangers.

I just kept swiping and talking to many people. At one point, I lost count.

The later the dates would last, the more seizure drugs I had to take, and the less I could speak clearly. Not only would I have trouble speaking, but I also had trouble thinking, likely due to the seizure drugs. I was yawning all the time during these dinner dates. It made it look like I was disinterested when I was absolutely interested.

The third date didn't go as well. The fourth, fifth, and sixth didn't go great, either. The girls knew something was wrong when I spoke. These girls had a multitude of options. Due to my illness, I lost my game. Or maybe I never had it. All of them told me there was no connection. I felt rejected again.

It had been a long time since I first began dating Maddie. Maybe I was out of practice or perhaps it was because I wasn't used to trying.

People dated for fun in their twenties. The people I dated in the past were not necessarily going to be the future for me. I didn't think that far ahead. I was dating just to date.

I felt like I'd never be wanted again after my diagnosis. I know friends who go through something similar after breakups. A breakup can mess with your system, sometimes permanently. I was already mentally and physically screwed up, but now I had to find someone who would accept me. I have constant seizures and cancer. Who would want to date me? The lack of companionship was another thing that sucked. I couldn't date, and if I did find someone, I'd have to tell them about my diagnosis. That lessened my chances.

I resorted to dating a former coworker who helped me get my first job and had already known about my diagnosis. She was happy to accept me. I couldn't believe it! She was a cool girl. But her brother was a hick, her father was on the opposite side of the political spectrum, and we just weren't compatible. It wasn't my ideal situation, but she still offered me a sense of comfort over years of being toyed with. This person brought me back to a sense of normalcy that I needed.

Her father came over one time unannounced, and I scrambled out of her bed. She was so nonchalant, and I was frazzled.

"I have to get up. It's not a good look," I said.

"No, I think he would just be happy to have his 32-year-old daughter in a relationship to get married."

That immediately turned me off. Marriage is a huge deal, and I had still not decided if I wanted to marry her. It was only after a few months. I was not going to be with someone desperate to marry any guy, no matter who they were. Apparently, I was either that guy who was the last option on their list of dating apps or a desperate attempt to land any guy. Maybe I misinterpreted the comment, but this was how I took it.

I thought about this situation a lot. She wanted to settle for anyone. I had more self-worth than that! The companionship was the only thing I got out of that fling.

I remember getting food from ShopRite when I got a text message. "Stop playing games with me." I had no feelings. Maybe I was a hypocrite for not wanting to be alone but being alone at the same time.

By now, I was over with love and thought I'd just settle for bachelor-hood. Again, why would anyone accept me? I didn't want someone to get too close to me for them to just experience a tragic loss. It was unfair to them. Dark thoughts entered my mind.

I sunk into a deep sadness. Lying in bed as much as I could was all I would do. I'd just lay there and stare up at the plain white ceiling, alone.

You wouldn't recognize me from the guy I used to be. I used to be smiling all the time. Now I was just a guy with a St. James bible by his nightstand who didn't know if he should believe anymore.

## MELANCHOLY MOMENTS

Kyle called just to check on me. The first thing he would always ask me, "Are you eating well." He is a person who truly cares about everyone else.

"They can go screw themselves," is his classic line for anyone who doubts my capabilities.

This man is one of my favorite former colleagues and best of friends. He has a beautiful son, wife, and life. He's always laughing, and deservedly so, as he would later rise to the top. He is the head medical director. There is no doubt in saying he was a big shot. But he is a guy with no ego and no self-entitlement—just a cheerful fellow. Kyle is one of the brightest people I have ever met.

"What's up, man? It's great to hear from you," I said, bursting with enthusiasm.

"Good to hear from you, brother. Just calling to check in on you. How are you feeling? Are you eating?" He's one of the few people who can ask that question.

"Good, good. My MRI came back clean."

"That's great! I always like to hear that."

We reminisced about all our times together.

"Remember that time in Boston. . ." or "Remember that time in Oslo. . ." or "Remember that time in Charleston. . ." or "Remember the first time we met. . ."

It's a shame we don't work together anymore because we don't keep in touch as often. I focus on all the stress that I have, and so does he. We were one of the closest on our team when we worked together. Coincidentally, Kyle gave me a book, The Emperor of All Maladies, right before my diagnosis. It was about the history of cancer. I still haven't finished it. It's been five years. The bookmark is still inside it just in case I have the urge to pick it back up and read. I don't think that urge will come anytime soon.

It had been a long time since I discussed the tumor with him in detail. I had been learning to deal with it at this point. I became comfortable speaking about it.

"It's what you do with this tumor that counts. It can be a blessing, but no matter what, it's God's plan. I don't know why it happens or what it means." That was a beautiful and humble admission of acceptance, I thought.

I imagined Kyle's reaction would be, "I can't believe how far you've come" or "What an amazing five years it's been. You've handled it all so well."

I've never heard him yell so loudly. At that moment, he was terrifying. "How can you say that? It's not a blessing. It's a curse. You're the best person I know!"

He told me he became an atheist because this had happened and that he didn't believe in God anymore. He never held back no matter how much I tried to reason with him.

"My religion teaches me that there are hard times, but God shows redemption for us all."

He responded, "If God loved you so much, how could I believe in him? There can't be a God."

I could tell that there was nothing I could do that would change his mind. I wanted to instill comfort in him by saying not to worry about me. I realized I was rattling off words. Just words. I wasn't even sure that I believed what I was saying. My faith was already waning.

I read the Gospel of John to see if I could get my faith back. It was going to take more than a few pages.

I could only pray. "Let me know if there's a meaning behind all of this."

# CHAPTER 5:

# BLESSINGS

With curses come blessings and vice versa. You may have to look past the silver lining. You might have to squint to see past all the evil that our illnesses may bring. I did not expect myself to ever face this situation. In pharmacy school, they taught us how to treat certain types of cancer, but they never taught us how to have it.

> *Every curse has a blessing, and every blessing has a curse.*
> *When you stand face-to-face with your destiny, will you be*
> *able to tell one from the other?*
>
> *—Author J.K. Ensley*

If you worked in a community pharmacy, CVS or Walgreens, you might have treated a few cancer patients and not even known. The thing we were robbed of in pharmacy school was the ability to speak to patients in these settings. A majority of time was spent wrestling with the insurance companies and maybe a few minutes throughout the day to speak to patients about their healthcare. The rest of the day was looking at the computer making sure the physician didn't mess up. That's it. No retail pharmacist has time to even look up at the patient. It was the same thing every day. I got burnt out after three years working in a retail pharmacy.

Being a retail pharmacist isn't as glorious as it seems.

When you work at a retail pharmacy and grab a prescription, you might notice the customer has cancer based on the medication prescribed. Then again, most oral medications are dispensed by a specialty pharmacy or are administered subcutaneously and some of them intramuscularly. But the majority are given in a hospital or an infusion center. These you cannot see from working in a retail pharmacy. There's no way to know for sure.

If you saw me right now—a backward hat, Invisalign, orange Tic Tacs, a designer shirt that in no way matches my joggers, and an old pair of Nikes on. . . you would form an opinion about me.

*Am I bumming out?*

*Do I not have style?*

*Could I be too lazy to have this appearance?*

*Would you guess that I'm a cancer patient—and how?*

Exterior looks versus interior thoughts.

## REBUTTAL

It took me a while to try to flip those curses into blessings. I still struggle with some and am constantly searching for a resolution with others. As I've said, with life comes hardships. That's the unforeseen beauty that life hands us.

Tough times will come your way. How do you deal with it? Soak in sorrow, or brush it off, or internalize it, or find a healthy way to release it.

You're not alone in your time of despair. You have never been nor ever will be. So, hearing Kyle's words was heart-wrenching. Hearing his raw emotions was painful. I hadn't realized the extent of the pain I cause people when others cry over me. It's been five years since my diagnosis and three years since I finished chemotherapy. This was how I envisioned life going forward. There was no reverse button on this, and frankly, I didn't want one. Five years later, it still seems unreal but acceptable. Sometimes I feel like I'm in a bad dream that I can't wake up from.

"Do unto others. That's what I believe. I only focus on helping people. The rest is up to God." This was my attempt to restore faith in Kyle.

I tried standing on my soapbox again. "We all hold power to positively affect people, from those who are sick or those who have unfortunately passed away." I was desperately trying to reach Kyle and make him understand that maybe there was a reason why God gave me this tumor.

He wouldn't buy it. He was mad at God. Or, even worse, he didn't even believe there was a God.

I didn't argue. Listening to his words was enough. When I first got diagnosed, I had to listen to every part of my being, which took a very long time.

So, I understood where he was coming from.

He must've thought I was still angry at God after those five years.

I still wanted Kyle to focus on the others afflicted with similar brain tumors, to express how fortunate I was to be alive. Don't get me wrong; I'm extremely happy to be where I am at thirty-three.

I feel guilty for not having glioblastoma. Why did I get the long end of the stick? Maybe it was the survivor's guilt coming out. But I've survived so long, in both age and diagnosis. Helping others through tough times makes me feel good about myself. Deep down, there has to be a reason I was struck with this disease. I had to figure it out.

I have a friend named Annabelle. Unfortunately, her father died last week. They were far by distance but close by heart. She gave the eulogy this morning. . . probably as I'm writing this all down. Annabelle's tragic loss should shake everyone who has lost a parent, whether you adored or despised them. I can't relate to having lost a parent. I could only offer my condolences and be there for her. But I couldn't speak to her about this, only listen. I hadn't experienced the same emotions that come with that sort of tragedy. I don't claim to know.

When loss of life occurs, I often hear, "They would have been proud" or "They would have wanted this for you."

I have no clue what Annabelle's relationship with her dad consisted of, but seeing how she took the loss, one might figure that out. I reached out and gave her the opportunity to tell her truth:

*There have been many blessings among these tragedies. My dad's very sick humor has kept me company since first being told of his passing by the funeral home, when they called to make arrangements. Since then, thinking in full sentences and delivery, the exact off-color comments he would be saying if he was here in the warm flesh, has kept me feeling close and in complicity with him. Sometimes I share these words out loud to friends and family, and we share in a full belly laugh. Apparently, my humor has captured more than just an essence of him.*

*Since his passing, it has become a priority of mine to honor him and his life by maintaining close relationships with his family, friends, and colleagues. In our developing friendships and closeness, we keep him alive. I remember people saying that time will heal this. I knew from the beginning that that would be the opposite for me. More time passing means that he has been dead for longer, that our memories together are further from my breath, and that I've had more memories that I'm unable to hear his reflection about in real life.*

*The pain and sadness around this immutable reality has changed me. It's made me say all that I want to in the moment with anyone, to put my phone down and be present with those in front of me, to stop pining to be with someone or somewhere*

*else when I am with myself or others. It has reminded me of the*
*suffering and sweetness of presentness.*

*While I acknowledge feeling freer from the weight of our*
*complicated father–daughter relationship, I miss my friend, and*
*I would do so much to have even the chance of our less good*
*moments together again.*

A few years ago, I was playing golf with a personal hero of mine, and he teared up when speaking about his parents. He said to me, "I can't wait to see Mom and Dad in heaven." This man was retired and possibly older or the same age when one of them died.

I told another man, "I was thinking of your parents today." I asked him, "Do you think of them?" He said, "Yes, every single day." His folks had died years ago, but the feelings never changed.

A handful of high school friends lost their parents, even the ones I speak with every day. One had deteriorating health issues, one had lung cancer, and another one died from COVID-19. I often wonder how my friends dealt with the loss. Obviously, they dealt with their loss in different ways. But to handle that so well on the outside was commendable. I'm sure there were *tears in the shower* moments behind the scenes. Maybe even some therapy. I think about how these tragedies affected others, namely their spouses.

Matt's mother was diagnosed with a tumor at a very early age, and she passed away much too soon. When I was going through chemotherapy. I asked about his mom's experience, out of curiosity and fear. I was trying to channel this energy. We chatted only for a few minutes. Then Matt put his head down because of either sadness or not wanting to talk. I felt bad that I brought that experience again.

I saw her shortly before she died. I was at his house, and I remember exactly where Matt, his father, and his mother were seated.

I kept thinking, would this be how I was to die, with people by my side, surrounded by love? Or was I to die alone? Would I die in pain? Would I die being on painkillers?

I tend to stop short of thinking about when death eventually comes for me.

## WONDERS IN FIGHTING

I bought a new home eventually. My office exudes a very serene feeling. There is a bookshelf resting on the floor. It contains all the books I received after my diagnosis and a large Claude Monet coffee-table book—my favorite painter.

It was graciously given to me by a former colleague.

The office has a flag hanging on the wall with all the people I honor who have had cancer. Past and present. The office also has all the prayer cards from funerals I've been to throughout the years. I have all my degrees and awards to let me know I am smarter than I feel.

I'll tell you my favorite thing about that office. When I stare above my computer screen, the decal that was ripped off the wall before I moved in says "Sparkles." I can see the shadow behind it. The previous owner had it hanging in his daughter's former bedroom. When I get overwhelmed at work, I look up, and that calms me down. It kept me sane during the lockdown and it brought a little smile to my face.

This whole twelve foot by twelve-foot room allows me peace. When I'm here, I strictly do work (hence the need for peace).

But I have these funky and random little things to keep me grounded. Sitting next to me, an inch away from my lorazepam, is a Rubik's cube. There's a funny lamp behind my monitors. On the opposite side, there is a Salvador Dali clock. There's also a framed picture of Jesus, Mary, and Joseph. And lastly, there is my mini-Eagles helmet. In my closet, I have six different Eagles jerseys hanging. There are autographed worn jerseys and helmets in my guestroom. I haven't tallied in a while, so there may be much more.

But the only thing that matters in my office, the foundation on which it was built, is a Venum boxing glove. It's just hanging by a string from a tack. Four degrees and only one of my awards I have hanging on the wall so I can leave room for the glove. It is mostly black with dark gold at the bottom. The boxing glove shows itself on every virtual call. I don't keep it as a memory for my oligo.

It has no deep meaning anymore. The real reason I keep it is for others—to recognize their battle for all the crap they face in life. I don't know what they are going through, but I assume everyone has something they are struggling with. It is part of my power. I want to encourage others to fight their own fight.

It's a reminder of others' pain. For example, there was so much I could do with those gloves but so little I could do to cure my cancer. My hope by doing this was to say, "Hey, it's not over"—to give someone else strength, a smile, or just say that someone is traveling along a path with something just as shitty.

One of my friends, Sean, was diagnosed with leukemia. He had lost thirty pounds and was being fed through TPN. His TPN was carried around and disguised as a book bag. It took me a little bit before I recognized his facial features. Sean was hunched over, struggling to make it inside my car, and whispered when he spoke because his lungs were sore. I brought up cheerful conversations because I knew from experience that being alone with your thoughts leads down a dark path.

When we got out of the car, I had to assist him. Again, I can relate to multiple instances of that. We had a quick dinner that night. But I couldn't get over one thing.

Sean and his wife had a baby two months prior. He was so immuno-compromised that he couldn't see his baby for the duration of chemotherapy. What happens if the baby gets sick? Would Sean react even worse?

He needed a bone marrow donor, but there were no matches for him. I wanted to help. There was nothing I could do.

If I could do anything physically to help him out, I would. But I tried in other ways. I unhooked my boxing gloves and gave one to him. Not the right glove, just the left. I figured he was a Southpaw. Fight the good fight. It was the least I could do on Christmas.

I've bought and sent boxing gloves to my friends who either had cancer or are grieving a loss due to this horrible disease.

I added a message. Each boxing glove reads "Grateful Mind, Peaceful Heart."

You may never win, but you'll certainly lose if you don't go down without a fight. It's so cliché, but I never understood it until a few years after my diagnosis. You need to trick yourself into believing it.

"I'm going to live forever." There truly is a psychological piece to brain tumors. Think positive, be positive.

A former colleague once told me, "Joey, don't be so self-deprecating—be positive." It was as if she was scolding me and I had only met her in person the day before.

But she was right. I was negative all the time, especially about my health, and she was teaching me how to act. I didn't realize how mean I was to myself, and maybe I had come across as this type of person. I couldn't even tell if I was kidding. Maybe I wasn't. This one girl completely changed my perspective on life. This is the way I hide my pain, I guess—being the total opposite of what I was trying to accomplish. I was a total fraud by preaching to the choir and not listening to the words myself.

My positivity came to fruition after that. I aspire to be like that on a full-time basis. When anybody insults themselves, I correct them. If a friend calls themself "Stupid," I say, "Tell yourself, 'I'm not stupid.'"

It is a ridiculous thing. I act sort of like their parent. But there is some reason for all of this. Reports have shown that positivity can change your outlook on life, especially when you recite it aloud. You begin to believe it. Any negative thing you say, it may become true—even when it's not true at all.

## LOOK ON THE BRIGHT SIDE

Work makes me angry, but I get paid to do it. My dog needs to go on a walk while I'm heavily asleep, but it forces me to get up and breathe in the crisp air. I wake up cranky in the morning, but I will feel better if I take fifteen minutes to do yoga. Bills sit on my counter, and I'm thankful that I have a counter to sit them on. I'm diagnosed with a terminal illness, but I take time to realize what good things exist in the world. I can sit and sulk or find a more positive option. I learned a lot as time went by.

Let me tell you about something pleasant that happened out of the blue over my diagnosis. My dad and uncle had not spoken for as long as I can remember. The only thing they had in common was me.

They'd walk by, even in the same house, and never say anything. Nothing at all. They didn't even speak at my grandmother's funeral. I have always been close with my uncle but didn't dare ask him why they ignored each other like ghosts. It was an unknown secret that only the Fulton brothers held. We are stubborn like no others. We are capable of holding grudges forever.

I had never found out why they didn't speak. Even my aunt didn't know about this when I asked her. From what I was told, it was about who their parents loved the most. I think my dad was closer to his father, and my uncle was closer to his mother. There was never any big blowout fight that happened between them. One day, they just stopped talking.

Then the next day, they resumed. It was after my brain surgery. My dad kept mentioning it to my uncle. Keeping him in the loop. He would obviously like to know about anything serious happening to his nephew. And this qualified. Once my father and uncle spoke, it was an instant bro-mance. . . all thanks to my diagnosis. They reconnected after all this time.

They text so much now, reaching out to each other all the time. Every time I stop over at my dad's house, it's always, "Did you text your uncle back? He said you haven't."

I knew it was real when they started smack-talking about me, jokingly, of course. Well, most of the time. If they were, in fact, gossiping, I would be so proud they formed as close of a relationship as Fulton's can have. Reconciliation is a big deal in our family.

The same thing happened with my sister and mom. They began reforming their relationship. I say *reform* because there are some things they'll never get over and moments that they'll never have back. Oh, and my sister and father! They had their issues they hopefully squashed.

I was so glad for those mending relationships, even if it came at my expense. If any type of change occurred from this tragedy—I'm delighted it was that.

There are hidden gems that can happen out of these types of situations. It has a way of bringing families together, and my family is an utterly dysfunctional one. Family is something that is precious. Time is always ticking. I hope every family can reconcile their differences.

This is something that you already know. You just need to have an action plan put together and hope that it is reciprocated.

## BROTHERS AND SISTERS

I'm guessing most of those with siblings can relate to this. You can absolutely love them! Or just tolerate them. . . loathe them. . . you might not speak to them, or whatever. In general, these are the people who can piss you off the most. Given this section, I felt it appropriate to mention how Sydney and I became close. . . how another person would CHANGE our lives and bring us back together.

I hadn't spoken to my sister for eight years. I saw on Facebook that my nephew was born, and I knew I would regret it if I had not been part of his life. I could not miss this moment.

One night I showed up at Sydney's door without warning and asked if I could hold my nephew. I showed up in the rain, not on purpose, but this was something that only occurs in movies.

This was less than two weeks after he was born. My wish to be an uncle outweighed the grudge I had against my sister. My nephew ended up being the force that brought my sister and me back into each other's lives.

There are regrets you can mend but not remove, some forgiven but never erased, and ones you're stuck with. Plenty exist in my past that I cannot return to because they have passed. We can take the experiences we've had, including those that haunt us, and learn to make peace with them.

## USE YOUR POWER

The most gratifying experience I've had from this tumor is my ability to network. I went searching on how to find that niche. It was my superpower. I was going to use the power. It was a damn good way to turn a tumor into a blessing.

That was the start of my journey with Imerman Angels, an organization for people not just with brain tumors, but any type of cancer. It's a website that matches you up with a mentor who has a similar cancer type, age, and sex. Having these one-on-one calls allows you to connect with someone who is in a similar situation as you. I would recommend this website to any cancer survivor out there, or rather, anyone who is experiencing a difficult disease.

Maybe you feel as if you can't confide in your partner, either due to embarrassment or because they aren't able to understand what walking in your shoes is like. You can find yourself having deep chats about health with someone who is going through or has been through cancer. You may even develop a friendship with them. Cancer creates a bond between strangers that you cannot change no matter how hard you try.

I signed up for Imerman Angels right before I started chemotherapy. I needed someone to vent to when I was going through these challenging and emotional times.

Todd was my mentor. He was from Chicago and a huge Bears fan. I was lucky to find a guy who was so down to earth. Todd was a cool guy who would tell it like it was with no sappy bullshit at all.

He had an interesting story. After a seizure that led to his diagnosis, his girlfriend of three years immediately left him when she learned about the tumor. He had to change jobs to ones that were less forward-facing because he could not speak as clearly. By that point, he had been diagnosed for three years and already had three craniotomies. It immediately struck me with fear. Was I going to have a craniotomy each year? The way he spoke was nonchalant. Like, it was life as usual.

"Does the tumor just grow into the cavity?" It seemed like such a scary experience for him to go through. I was curious from an intellectual perspective and less from my emotions.

"Yup, they snip it out." His response fascinated me.

He said it with such confidence, too. He was acting like this tumor was no big deal to him. And I could tell it was genuine!

"What was chemotherapy like?"

"You'll have your days when you throw up a ton. A lot of nausea. Other than that, you are fine."

He took Temodar and still dropped a lot of weight. "It worked really well as a weight loss program for me. The chemotherapy helped me hit my BMI goal."

He helped prepare me through every step of the "having cancer" process. It was also him subliminally giving me the worst-case scenario for everything so I wouldn't be surprised. Finally, someone knew exactly what was on my mind and what I was going through—someone who could mean it when he said, "Having cancer fucking sucks." There was no emotion behind it, because we were the ones who were dealing with the exact same thing. That bond formed and forced us together.

It wasn't until I was done with chemotherapy and in a good headspace that I became a mentor for Imerman Angels. My first mentee was Dylan. He was a very nice, respectful man who would resort to texting because he was having problems with his speech.

He was dealing with a great deal of depression and suicidal thoughts that he expressed to a medical professional. He could not work anymore because of his seizures and had to live at home. His tumor was in the front of his head, so his scar was impossible to hide. Imagine the looks that people gave him, staring at the scar way before looking him in the eyes.

Dylan was a tough mentee to start with, and I'm not sure I helped him as much as Todd helped me. A tumor can make up a small or large percentage of your life. It all depends on how much you let it. I'll admit my life seemed way easier than his by the initial reaction I got from Dylan. But I didn't have the intention of judging someone else's cancer. "Your cancer is worse than my cancer" is not a road anyone should go down.

Imerman Angels are about listening, sharing experiences, and talking through similar things you both have been through. Dylan had been recently diagnosed and was still in the grieving process. I only had the right to support and root for him.

My second mentee was Sophia. Her story felt far different from Dylan's. She had previously got engaged to her boyfriend of seven years. However, a brain tumor changed the plans she had with her fiancé. She felt as if she was letting him down by being diagnosed with cancer, sort of like making him be her caretaker. But Sophia was lucky, as he was in it for the long haul. This secretly made me jealous because of what happened to me and Maddie.

Sophia's mom was also dying from breast cancer, creating a rush to have her present for the ceremony. All of her emotions came out at once. Understandably.

Sophia had also undergone radiation, so her hair was falling out. Every time we spoke, she would ask how long her hair would take to grow back.

"Would it grow back quicker?" Sophia was researching scalp tips and tricks and asking a person who uses 2-in-1 shampoo and conditioner. I could only tell her about my own experience. Naturally, she was torn between wearing a wig or getting married bald. I could hear in her voice that her fiancé was consistently supportive of whatever choice she made.

She ended up sending me pictures of her wedding. Sophia got married with a wig, while on chemotherapy, with her mother present.

Mentoring Michael left an impression on me. He is a unique individual; he's open, honest, and doesn't give a damn what people think of him. I was sitting calmly on my porch during our first FaceTime call. I immediately saw the pain in his eyes. I'd give everything to take the tears away if I could. He was just like me when I received my diagnosis. I saw myself in Michael and felt the exact same way when I had my first call with Todd.

He was at the lowest point in his life. Michael lost his job and had to move back into the home of his fiancé's parents. There was tension between the couple. I told him it was okay to grieve. "That's what you're supposed to do."

I asked if he cried every day. "Yes."

I could relate.

It was like looking in the mirror at myself.

It brought back those terrible memories.

It's all about the process. I wanted to ask these personal questions related to his brain tumor. He was looking for someone else to feel like he wasn't alone. Although I'm a couple of time zones away, I was his mentor who was going through the same thing. "You're not alone in this," I felt like pleading.

I gave Michael my main piece of advice that I attempt to give others: "If others try to help, just let them. It's not for you; it's for them. Will your fiancé appreciate that? If so, then let her help."

Over time and through regular conversations, he achieved acceptance and pure happiness. He got married, found a new job and a new home, and his doctor reassured him the tumor was completely resected. From our first FaceTime call to where he is now, his *new* life has changed for the better. It's weird calling him my mentee anymore. He has undoubtedly become more than that—my friend.

Someone had reached out to him asking for a testimonial about Imerman Angels. I was astonished by the power of his words. I cried that I had an effect on someone. He shared them with me:

*I found myself talking to people in my life that can't relate to my diagnosis of Anaplastic Oligodendroglioma. I felt alone in that sense, even while having all the support in the world.*

*Having a mentor angel with a similar diagnosis to me has been the most incredible and unique experience I could have asked for.*

*At the time I was going through treatment, I was also unemployed. I experienced a lot of depression, and my angel assured me never to be afraid of asking for help and being vulnerable. I was told by my angel to use all my resources and take advantage of every opportunity. Little did I know that at the end of it all, I would find a job I am in love with.*

*Imerman Angels have taught me how to grieve in a healthy way and cope with the loss of my old self. Ever since my diagnosis, I knew that I would never be the same, but I have learned to be a new and improved version of myself. My angel expressed to me that I am a warrior and I have the fight in me unlike any other person, and for that, I am forever grateful.*

*It's so nice to have someone to talk to who has been through a similar experience because other people in your life have most likely not been through this cancer. It was incredibly beneficial to talk through radiation stories, chemotherapy stories, surgery stories, etc. My angel and I were able to make each other laugh and make each other cry through it all. This experience allowed me to know I can get through this cancer and make it out of it as a better person.*

Michael has helped me more than I have helped him.

I was the guest speaker at an event for the American Brain Tumor Association and told the shortened version about my journey with cancer thus far. I was quite amazed to speak about cancer without anybody being uneasy about the word. It allowed me to speak freely in terms that everybody could relate to. Guilt kicked in once again. I see all the people with worse types of brain cancer than I have. I was comparing once again. What type of brain cancer do they have?

Was I the youngest person in this room?

Witnessing people who were worse off than myself pushed all my grandstanding aside and left me feeling humbled. Some couldn't comprehend anything because of the effects of radiation. Some couldn't even speak. There were a lot of people there with glioblastoma. Many families of those who passed even showed up. They proved that this disease formed a strong connection filled with so much support.

I had little to say in terms of my experience. I was so new to this. But everyone opened their arms to welcome me into the family. The patients and staff attended this event year after year. I had another family to join.

## FRIENDS ARE FOREVER

At this point, I was so used to opening up about my diagnosis. I felt comfortable doing a roundtable presentation when I was asked. It's easy to talk honestly about questions that come from a close friend—just a casual conversation. That's the approach I used when going into this roundtable. It was as if we were in a coffee shop together, and he was asking about my brain tumor for the first time, the only difference being there were hundreds of people in attendance. But I was familiar with the setting from previous talks I've done.

After the talk and the Q&A came around, I had relevant questions that had to do with the presentation and the pharmaceutical industry.

"What does your disease state need currently?" One of the attendees asked. I could tell she was inquisitive.

"Helpful resources for patients. Both informative and supportive, especially for the caregiver."

Then came the most awkward question.

Another woman asked, "With your brain tumor, do you ever think about the future or your prognosis?"

It took me a second to process this question. And this time, it wasn't due to what I thought the Q&A was supposed to be. The audience went quiet.

Who would ask that? The awkwardness was humorous to me. I can't really remember what I said immediately after. I was still trying to interpret the question.

What was she trying to ask?

Was she asking, "What do you want to accomplish before you die?"

So, I just rambled on.

I said something about the need for additional mechanisms of action, a road trip to New Mexico, and more FDA-approved drugs. Just anything to avoid the question. I spoke about the need for clinical trials. As I said, I just rambled on about anything and everything, even if it made no sense.

Then I took it very deep. I knew that would be my last question. Who could follow that question up?

"I can beat this. Ninety-nine percent of patients may pass, but I could be that one percent who survive." I meant it. "When you read through a study, just realize we are more than just a number. There are patients behind that number." I was getting very passionate.

Whatever was on my mind, I just released it all. Then, I walked off.

Nearly five years later, I went to New Mexico. People often ask me why. I have been there a few times, most recently attending the Albuquerque Balloon Fiesta. Another time, I went to visit a previous ex-girlfriend for a summer internship. And the other, I went for a work conference. I love New Mexico because it is the opposite of the hustle and bustle in my home-town. It's my own getaway destination to enjoy the quietness and the small buildings. New Mexico is my safe haven.

I was celebrating these five years of hell by purposely being in iso-lation. But I had to do it with my friend Rachel. She always asked, "When are we going to New Mexico?" It was her way of saying, "You said you were going to do it; now do it." I finally got off my ass and made it happen.

When I texted her, she already knew. "New Mexico." I gave her five days' notice.

It was my birthday during that brief stint. My phone was turned off. I felt the need for peace. So, I went on that trip and didn't tell anyone except Rachel. I needed this for myself, and I needed to do this with her.

# CHAPTER 6:

# JACK

My neuro-oncologist recommended I see a therapist as soon as I came out of complete shock. At the time, there was so much going on that we would have to deal with the physical things first, like attempting to restore my right-side weakness that was a result of the surgery. That was my dominant hand. There was no chance of throwing a baseball or football straight anymore. They spun right into the ground. Turns out that occupational therapy could do nothing to fix it. Oh, and my peripheral neuropathy—no taking that vincristine back.

*Hands* was in the running to be the name of this chapter. But I don't have enough content. I mean, a couple of paragraphs is all. And *Helplessness* seems like the whole theme of this book.

I was stumped.

But the theme of hell is a perfect way to start this chapter. I've been through it all, in more ways than one. Many, many ways. . . I was mentally messed up.

> *"Honesty gets us sober, but tolerance keeps us sober."*
>
> —*Dr. Bob Smith*

I had to think with objective measures and turned to someone I trusted when I committed to starting therapy. I tend to make impulsive decisions when I commit to anything. Kyle was the smartest guy I knew. I mean, c'mon, he's a PhD in the neuroscience therapeutic area. His position is a few steps away from the chief medical officer. I respected his insight from an objective point of view.

I asked him, "What's worse: losing your body or your mind?"

Without hesitation, he said, "Your mind." I think this was from him having a background in neuroscience.

I couldn't even differentiate what it felt like to have mental distress back then. I'd never been to therapy because I preferred suppressing the demonic memories down until they eventually burst out into flames. That was my concept of how life was. I had a lot of friends but really didn't open up to anyone about my past. They only knew parts of my life that I allowed them to see.

My life was a secret. They knew bits and pieces. Not even my closest friends knew about the entire thing—never the whole story, and God forbid anything emotional. Because I didn't bring up my past, friends wouldn't dare ask. Going through my "crying every day" phase made me rethink the situation. My "burst" was eventually going to have to come out.

These thoughts affected my recovery just as the mind and body are physically connected. One thing goes with the other. So, Kyle was wrong; it was both. A body can't exist without a mind, and a mind is useless without a body.

This entire time I worried about the tears that ran down my face.

Maybe they were the wrong tears, coming from a "woe is me" attitude.

Or maybe that's why I laughed when the doctor called me to inform me of this diagnosis. Could it be my twisted sense of humor? Or was it something else?

Maybe that's why I thought, this isn't even the hardest thing I've been through.

I could've handled the tumor better if things hadn't come to a head all at once. The thermometer was filled up with mercury. It reached its boiling point and exploded. It may have done so eventually.

Maybe the tumor was a good thing for me. Cancer led me to attempt therapy.

It could have been a hidden sign that I needed help.


## MAN WITH A FISH

I chose a therapist as far away from the cancer center campus as possible. That forty percent resection still terrified me. I wanted to separate my life from the tumor—give it some distance. I didn't want to see that building every day. I'd rather pay for an Uber even if it was thirty minutes away. At least it was in the opposite direction of that damn hospital.

Finding a great therapist is hard to find for everyone. My friends would tell me to go to multiple therapists until I found someone that I clicked with. Matchmaking is really what it is. I was mentally exhausted over the whole Maddie situation, so I didn't have the energy to look for a therapist more than once. If the first one was unsuccessful, I would just give up for a period of time. I had neither the energy nor the time to find another.

I went through my preferences by looking at the area I chose. It was a sort of algorithm that had met a certain criterion. First, I wanted a male. The reason why I wanted this is I don't want to swear in front of women. I'm sure they are used to it. But for me, I would feel uncomfortable with that. That's not the way my mom raised me. She used to say, "Never use foul language in front of a woman. Save it for the boys. You're allowed to do that."

The other reason for this part of the algorithm is that they had to exist in my preferred area. There are very few male therapists.

The final piece to this algorithm was that they had to be in network for insurance purposes.

Meeting a therapist for the first time was awkward because we would be discussing ME. I was okay with mentoring or supporting others. When it came to focusing on my feelings, it felt unnatural. When I spoke at all those events, it was different. It excited me to talk about my journey through cancer. But going into my personal secrets with someone I don't know was very scary. I didn't know what my expectation was. Do I tell this guy all there is to know about me?

I chose a guy named Jack. I must admit I felt skeptical about him.

Was he a *Soprano's* type or a *Good Will Hunting* type of therapist? Would he just listen or have conversations with me? How many times would he ask, "How does that make you feel?"

So, choosing Jack was going to be an equally challenging task for both of us. We'd have to figure each other out. My personality is difficult to adjust to at first, but once people figure me out, they know the real Joe—just not anything hiding deep down inside me.

In my first session with Jack, he laid out the rules. This guy was already intimidating, and I couldn't push back because of my speech. And I didn't have the energy to push back because I didn't care about much of anything anymore.

"What's your goal for therapy?" He'd have to convince me that this wasn't a waste of time, and I'd have to convince him that I bought into this idea.

"My doctor said I should go."

He probably wanted me to say, *I need to work on myself* or something, but I showed a lack of enthusiasm. I'm sure people come with emotional thoughts that they want to get out. I would eventually get there, but I was still a rookie at this. But one thing really caught my attention.

Jack had a black Betta fish named Carl that spent most of the time staring at the same plastic plant and pirate ship. I pondered how boring it must be swimming around in a tiny fish tank. That was Carl's life; he did that the entire day and night. Then I remembered that he had no memory. He was a fish, ugly as ever. But I couldn't figure out why he would be in a therapist's office.

He was right next to Jack. Carl was just so distracting for me that sometimes I would get annoyed at him being there. So, there I was, a few minutes into the session, ticked off by a fish. Maybe I needed therapy after all.

The more visits we had, the more comfortable I felt to open up. Jack didn't pressure me. Most of the beginning conversations I had were tumor-related. That's all he knew about me, and I wasn't about to give him anything else to psychoanalyze just yet. Oftentimes, I give away more health-related information than I should. I didn't open up much about my seizures. But we had an hour together each session, once a week. We'd have to come up with something to talk about.

I was dreading therapy sessions at the start of the week, then looking forward to them the day before. I'd need to set the agenda for the day. Enough time had passed, and I began to spend plenty of energy on Maddie. Talking shit about Maddie was low-hanging fruit I'd save for another time. Impending doom was what I wanted to talk about—just death and dying.

Months went by, and I kept thinking about it. With all these medications going in my stomach and all these lines constantly running through my veins, it's hard not to think about death. I was relying on these things to live. I could also use these things to die. They controlled my life. I started to notice that Jack understood more of the thoughts going through my head.

The conversations went pitch dark quickly. Jack knows when I'm on a specific topic just to ride it out. Jack grew up a catholic, so I knew he'd be on the same playing field as me. We believed in heaven and hell. I asked him impossible questions such as "What's heaven like?"

He didn't know; he hadn't been there. My wish was that he'd say, "It's glorious, a beautiful place, and you'll be happy when you get there," just so I could be reassured. It was all a big fantasy speech.

I became obsessed. He knew as much as I did about whether heaven and hell were really as they were depicted in the Bible. According to whatever religion you believe in, they'll tell you what it is, as if describing it to you.

His office became my new safe place, besides my shower, to cry it all out. I figured out that there were multiple levels of my grief I had hidden away. Sometimes one would have to dig far down. If you dug down deeper, you'd hit something else. It was the first time that I fully opened up about my past.

There are those who assume this book's primary purpose is about a brain tumor. And I hope that means so much to those readers. The central reason to write about this was cancer, but the real reason is something else. I needed to write this down for something else. I was most likely going to trash it after. I just had to get it out.

I was scarred before.

My brain is forever wired to be the sweet guy. The nice guy. The "I'll take good care of your daughter". . .and then actually do it. I was afraid of conflict. I was very straight-edge. It all started with my mom. I refuse to hold her anything but dearly. That was her molding me into the image of God.

By the time I was ten, I had begun to pick up on some things. I started to notice the world wasn't perfect when my mom acted differently. She fell down the stairs. She had a bad seizure and a busted eye from it. She passed out on the couch every night. She dismissed every alcohol binge as her being Irish.

We've all heard the association between being Irish and alcohol, but this was a mental illness. This was something you couldn't ignore, slowly unraveling itself into something you fear the most. My sweet mother.

## HAZY

She left me when I was fifteen. My mom is the person I love the most, even now. It took a long time to forgive. Years had gone by that we couldn't get back. She still texts or calls me every now and then, but that's it. I don't open up about her, and people do their best to ignore it. Even in intimate relationships, I never give out many details.

Part of me is ashamed, part of me is embarrassed, and part of me is damaged. It's damaged so bad that I block it out from my mind. I go weeks without thinking about her. And it's sad when I do. When I think of her, a sense of anxiety pops up.

It was alcohol and depression that drove her away. It was a crazy time in that house. She used to drink so much that she would lie on the couch with wine in hand. Every night. I couldn't take the stumbling, falling, and seizures she was having. It was too much for a teenager to take. I felt bad, then angry. She would speak to her mother, who was a drunk as well, every single night. My grandma's husband would curse me out on the phone for doing nothing.

My mother would make up stories about me that weren't true. Meanwhile, I'm eating TV dinners, hotdogs, and spaghetti every single night. She didn't eat yet managed to get her calorie intake from wine. There were nights when she would drink over half a bottle of wine. If she would stay up later, the whole bottle. Every time she went grocery shopping, there were a bunch of bottles of wine packed in the bags.

It's sad to think of us being broke because of alcohol. There were a couple of hundred dollars of wine in those bags that could've been used on rent. My mom had to move yearly because she couldn't pay off the bills. One winter, we had to turn the heat off and sleep in two pairs of pajamas. I didn't fully understand it at the time. It was alcoholism, and it is not a good situation to be around.

She was my biological mother. But this person wasn't my mom anymore. She was this malevolent creature who was the opposite of the lovely woman I had grown up with. People sometimes pass their scars down to another. I'm scared of being like her in terms of alcohol. That's the reason I will never drink alone. I'm so afraid that I will become an alcoholic.

Somedays, I would fantasize about suicide but didn't have the guts to follow through with it. I thought about it a whole lot, though. I had a lot of demons even back then. I didn't know what kind of mother I would have that day. Would it be the mother who would give me a kiss goodnight, or the *fake mom,* who would leave without feeding me? I had to take a few dollars from my allowance for lunch the next day.

This *fake mom* would mess up any child who was still growing and their brain developing. Meanwhile, I was getting straight A's, teachers loving me, being the ideal child because I needed that self-validation.

## ANGELS

Twenty-four trap on one. It was by far the simplest play in the playbook. A straightforward quarterback handoff to the running back, splitting right between the center and right guard. We were running that play over and over the whole game. One player was expecting it. I lowered my shoulders; he went lower than me. And the remainder of that play is how I faced a picture-perfect back injury.

That injury manifested into two herniated discs that required surgery. It messed everything up: my legs are different sizes, my feet aren't aligned, I'm living with scoliosis, and I still get weekly massages to this day for my tight muscles trying to hold my body up. And it happened at the right time. It was a perfect time to have your mother get up and leave.

Unbeknownst to me, my mother went and asked my sports coach, Anthony, as her only option to take me in. No one else. She had already made the decision to move separately, to get away from me, and move to a faraway state with my grandma. She was purposely leaving her son behind.

This makes me sound like a horrible child. Ask any one of my friends and they'll tell you differently. Ask people who are not my friends, and they'll say, *at least he's a nice guy*. I don't have any enemies.

I came to find out the real story of where I eventually landed—*grew up*, is a better term. If my memory serves me right, Anthony had asked a few families to take me in—they all declined. My mom had a move-out date already planned. Urgency had already begun.

I arrived at the hospital for my spinal surgery. Anthony had it out with Sydney for not taking me into her and her boyfriend's apartment. Anthony, somehow, got involved in taking care of me. He was the only person who cared for me at that time.

The last memory I have of my mother was sitting in my recovery bed, with her sitting in the chair, awkwardly, and us watching a runaway police car chase on the news.

Mom. . . even *fake mom*. . . only declined quicker.

Next thing I remember after that was Anthony telling me I was going to live with his parents.

"Staying with my parents will be good for them!"

Anthony was one of six, with a whole bunch of nieces and nephews.

A good ol' Catholic family.

Behind the scenes, it took a great deal of convincing before his parents came around to the idea.

He told me, "It is great for them to have you. They can raise a kid all over again."

I don't know how he made that happen, or why. I'd like to think he saw some promise in me. That he saw hope in me. That someone, besides my father who lived two hours away, wanted to care for me because he couldn't. I'll always love my mom. These are just the facts.

## THE IDEA OF DINNER

I was in the hospital having my spinal surgery and wound up recovering in the home of Anthony's parents. This wasn't the ideal childhood upbringing to say the least. It's not like it was wrist surgery or an ACL tear. I had back surgery, so I was mostly confined to a bed for a week. I don't remember much because of the painkillers. Haunted by evil thoughts I stored inside to figure out what I was in.

This was my substitute family now. I had elderly people walking by my door. Strangers to me. I didn't even know their first names for a while. I addressed them as Mr. and Mrs. Henderson. They must've been in their seventies. A fifteen-year-old waking up in the morning—it would affect anybody's psyche. I was so unaware, and living in my sports coach's old home made it even weirder.

What was the alternative? Sleep at the YMCA? I guess the powers that be would take me into child protective services. I don't know any other way to put it but childhood abandonment. It's hard to even talk about it now, to read these words. I can't even see that situation happening to anyone else.

What if I finally mustered up the courage to kill myself? Being told I was the problem in someone's life—that would kill most people, at least inside. It would be the perfect opportunity to do it right then and there. But I remember one thing. I had a better-than-normal life being with the Hendersons.

"Joe, are you ready for dinner?" Mrs. Henderson asked.

That was the first time I had a sit-down meal in such a long time. There I was, sitting at a dinner table being served by Mrs. Henderson. I didn't know how to react. And Mr. and Mrs. Henderson said the rosary every night with or without me. If I hadn't joined them, I would have been on AIM, MySpace, or doing homework. I was given the freedom to do whatever I wanted.

They got me a job at their church's rectory; sometimes the priest would hand me money under the books. The Hendersons were more than Anthony's parents to me. They were saints. What was this? I hadn't experienced love since the time Mom used to tuck me in every night when I was ten years old. I experienced love automatically with Mr. and Mrs. Henderson while Mom was living with my grandma several states away.

I struck gold with the Hendersons, more than I could ever imagine. I wondered at the time if this was how everyone grew up. I felt loved again. It was a feeling that I had missed. I was being cared for. There was breakfast served before I got ready for school, lunch packed in tin foil, and supper on the table every night. Anthony's parents and I became close. Especially Mrs. Henderson. Spending all the time I had with her makes me happy enough to cry. I still think about them daily.

I spoke to Anthony almost two decades later about what would have happened if he hadn't set me up to live with his parents. I personally think that I would've turned out to be a bad kid, one who resented life and never gave it a fair chance because of what happened to me. I may have become more jaded though, which ended up happening. But what if my mom stayed? What kind of child would I become?

My mom missed several pivotal moments in my life. She used to tell me, "High school is going to be the best time in your life." Mom was dead wrong; they were the worst years. In high school, Mr. and Mrs. Henderson had kept me alive. And I had kept my high school friends and made new friends through the Henderson family. For the first time, I wouldn't have to take public transportation. Mrs. Henderson drove me everywhere she was comfortable with. I had no cares in the world. I did all the usual things that kids do in high school, or what they are supposed to be doing. I felt like I fit in and almost spoiled because I had never experienced that treatment before. The only suggestion was that I go to church with them. They never forced me though.

In a way, they helped restore my faith in God. For Christmas, Mr. and Mrs. Henderson gifted me Rosary Beads. They hang in my bedroom to this day.

The Hendersons were a part of the most special moments of my life. They were there when I opened my college acceptance letter, prom, and my graduation. They were also there for my embarrassing moments. Mrs. Henderson always dropped me off and picked me up at the front entrances at dances. This is every high schoolers' nightmare.

The saddest moment was when I moved out shortly before college. I can remember Mr. Henderson, not a man of many words, but instead, hugged for the first time. Watching Mrs. Henderson cry at the front door made me want to run back inside. I thought about not leaving but the next stage of life was soon beginning.

I was still a kid socially developing. They knew the proper way to raise a child who has gone through immense trauma.

It wasn't until my college years that I'd visit them from my car window. It was a two-hour drive to watch them eat dinner from the car. I couldn't bring myself to go in. I was so overcome with emotions. Call me a spy. Call me a creep. I had every intention to go in. Every bone in my body was ready to sit down with them but as Kyle said, the mind wouldn't let me. They just wouldn't line up. That brought back a hectic yet sad time in my life, so I would just drive away. One day I felt brave enough to knock on their door to say one final hello. It soon became a goodbye.

The only funerals I had ever cried at were theirs. They were a blessing; they were my angels. I think about them constantly. I wish I could thank them one last time.

*2 Corinthians 4:15-18*

*All this is for your benefit, so that the grace that is reaching more and more people may cause thanksgiving to overflow to the glory of God. Therefore, we do not lose heart. Though outwardly we are wasting away, yet inwardly we are being renewed day-by-day. For our light and momentary troubles are achieving for us an eternal glory that far outweighs them all. So we fix our eyes not on what is seen, but on what is unseen, since what is seen is temporary, but what is unseen is eternal.*

## RECONCILIATION

I reconnected with my mom seven years later. She fought with her mother, sister, brother, friends, and two boyfriends in that span while being an alcoholic. They all shut her out. After seven years you start to forget about a person. In my case, this was my own mother. There was no dealing with an alcoholic. Even some people kept enabling her drinking habits. I heard very minor details of what was going on when she was away, but my concern was focused on my own career aspirations.

I was in pharmacy school and still working a forty-hour per week job. I had no time. My mind was consumed. My sister had gotten married, so Mom missed that, too. Sydney built a family. For my mom, I have no clue what she did in that period. . . other than some low-end jobs based on her LinkedIn profile. And I probably don't want to know any of the details.

It would be bad for me to digest her thoughts at that point in time. We all knew she was an alcoholic. But did she know? It's a shame. There was no convincing my mother then.

Finally, she had gone to rehab to reach sobriety, and I thought we could rehash our relationship now that she was going through the 12-Step Program. My mom was doing good. She was no longer the *fake mom* that I once knew. The alcohol altered her brain a little bit, but for the most part, she was all there. I loved having my *true mom* back again.

"Once an alcoholic, always an alcoholic," she once told me—an acknowledgment and acceptance of her problem. She used to send me her chips. A chip is one of the things that her center does. One chip represents being one month sober. Being six months sober, one would receive another chip. The happiest moment of my life was when she mailed me her one-year chip. I remember that exact moment. I called her.

"I'm so proud of you! You made it. Now it's on to make it two chips—two years sober."

Shortly after, she relapsed and became the same *fake mom* as before. We would only connect after my dog Hailey died. I sent her money for the dog's funeral. It was really my dog, but I couldn't bring a pet to the Hendersons'. She never paid me back, which didn't surprise me. Then periodically she asked for money, which I gave her because she was still my mom. I was a true momma's boy.

I finally had no choice but to cut her off financially. I put an end to the pity money and encouraged her to get a job, which she eventually lost because she showed up drunk. She was a poor soul. I wasn't physically there, couldn't stop her from drinking, and needed to recognize she was an adult and not a child.

But I still do love her. I've forgiven her. I'm also a grown man. And my money must start going toward student loans.

Being so emotionally damaged, this affected the trajectory of my life. It affected my ability to love and care. I would push away any woman who ever loved me. Once women got too close, I'd wipe them from memory and never look back. I would immediately shut off any feelings from them.

## THE TURNAROUND

It wasn't until I matured and let my guard down that I was able to accept Maddie into my life. And then I met Jack, to dig up those feelings and realize what I was keeping hidden down. My breakup with Maddie, which led to my relationship with Jack, was the best thing for me. I finally forgave Maddie after years of realizing her manipulation.

When Maddie texted me that she recently got engaged, on my *craniotomy anniversary* of all days—that's when I knew I had no feelings for her. That didn't affect me either way. I didn't care.

The most important thing that Jack taught me was to love myself. It took thirty years and a whole lot of tears, stress, and self-hatred. I always focused on others and neglected myself.

Concentrating on others' needs became a ritual, an obsession. I didn't know how else to live life. Through the process with Jack, I realized that I previously hated everything about life. When you hit rock bottom, you come out stronger.

"I don't matter; others matter." I had a way of dismissing my self-worth." It was the hardest internal battle I've faced. I previously discovered I was focused on making other people happy as my joy in life. Doing things for myself had finally made me blissful. Jack is responsible for my self-love. Not any girl. Not my friends. Just him.

I would go on these long tangents about some nonsense topic. Jack would call me out. "You are being a bullshitter." And this is not a negative comment. I respond better when he's being real. You have to become my friend first, someone I trust, before I open up about my life. I had, or maybe still have, imposter syndrome. I always have things to work on. I've been through a lot of shit, handled more than I ever could as a boy and a man, and accomplished too much with the cards I've been dealt.

## COMFORT

Relationships were a big topic I spoke about with Jack. I just needed comfort in my life instead of being alone in an empty home. I needed unconditional love. Even if I was not dating, I needed to be okay with myself. I cried so much in his office that I used to bring in a box of tissues just in case. It turns out that I was still grieving.

I used to fight through things to shake off the grief. I was the Superman that can overcome my grief with time and patience. Since I am forever attached to this brain tumor, Jack suggested that I give it a name. If I was Superman, who is the enemy of Superman—Lex Luther. Whenever I meet with him, Jack will always refer to the tumor as Lex.

I am working on getting "I'm not worthy" out of my lexicon. I can and will survive to the best of my abilities. I will fight Lex to the death. And if I die, he will die. But at least he'll go down with me.

## WHAT HAS BECOME

Enough time has gone by that I've come to the realization that the tumor is only a minuscule part of my life. Living with Lex is an annoyance that I'll never get rid of no matter how hard I try. I attempt to not focus on him. The focus on faith was very important to me. I speak a lot in this book about regaining my faith in God. I don't want to lose that.

It's hard for some people to find God, maybe even just a belief in God. Jack would tell me what he believed, but only when I probed. Jack taught me facts only a certain number of people would know. He wouldn't sway me in either direction when it came to faith. He let that be my decision. I appreciate him for letting me have a choice in it.

I always look forward to my meetings with Jack. It has become my favorite part of the week. And I still shed a tear occasionally because I'm still going through a whole bunch of topics on a week-by-week basis.

I even forgave Carl for being a fish. I'd always say "Hi" to him before I even greeted Jack. He heard my stories from a distance, separated by a fish tank. R.I.P. Carl.

# CHAPTER 7:

# TWENTY-SIX DAYS

July 2022. Lex just wouldn't go away. It became an everyday thing—clutching onto my head as if I was having a massive migraine. Something was up. It felt like Lex was growing back. MRIs didn't show it, but clinically there was something going on inside my head. I had headaches for months, and I never had them in the past. I didn't even keep a stash of Tylenol anywhere. I didn't need it until recently. Also, the most precious thing, my mind, was slowly erasing itself. All these things happened quite suddenly.

If I were to say something embarrassing, I'd clutch. If I were to do something embarrassing, I'd clutch. If I were to forget a simple word, I'd clutch.

I was the person that people looked up to, and I tried desperately to force myself to be positive. Not to be a hero, but to show others I could lead a normal life while dealing with Lex.

I've gotten used to my body failing me. This time my belief was that I was failing my body. When I was diagnosed the first time, I prayed, "Give me five more years of normalcy."

I asked for only five years. Maybe I should've asked for more.

I expected to go back under the knife, like Todd did. Seizure activity had increased in frequency, which made the decision easier to make. My epileptologist was maxing out on every single dose of the five drugs I was on, and the seizures still wouldn't stop. Fortunately, my neuro-oncologist knew a highly regarded brain surgeon who dealt with my primary issues: speech and seizures. I did a lot of research on him beforehand, and these complications were his bread and butter. Most importantly, he was on the other side of the country. He was far, far away from the surgeon who worked on my initial surgery.

The primary goal of the surgery was to reduce my seizure medication. The secondary goal was to scrape any more of the cancer away while he was in my brain. Whatever—he couldn't make me worse.

"Can you use your connections to bump me up in the process?" I said to my neuro-oncologist.

Working in healthcare, nothing ever gets done on time. This time it did. I was to see the surgeon in three weeks. This was lightning speed for an elective brain surgery. I booked my flight with that mentality.

There were a few more reasons why I needed the surgery. I lost a job over a seizure while interviewing with another company. I had already received an unofficial offer from them. Since COVID-19 restrictions lightened up, representatives from the company wanted to meet me in person. I flew down to Georgia and had lunch with the manager and senior director. Then it struck: a seizure.

They looked at each other. They didn't know what was going on with lip my twitching. I had no choice but to hide my twitch. I got up and made my way toward the bathroom to ride it out.

What started off as a wonderful interview had ended badly. When I returned home and reached out to Human Resources, they ghosted me. They immediately reposted the position and began reinterviewing. I needed to find a silver lining in all of this. Maybe another surgery would buy me more time to live? Maybe this would cure my seizures? I had all these people praying for me, and clearly these prayers had not worked. Was I an "everything happens for a reason" type of person?

Before the surgery, I had to travel across the country for a single night to have an electroencephalogram (EEG). It was a way to measure seizure activity. Somehow the doctor could pinpoint the area in the brain that targets the seizure origin before he would put the electrodes on the tissue. It was a pre-op before the actual surgery.

The result was a bunch of lines on a paper for the surgeon. Honestly, I didn't care about the test. It was just part of the process I had to complete. I was very prepared after going through the hell of the first surgery to know all the lingo. I was fascinated by the science, nonetheless.

To my surprise, Anthony was in the area at the exact same time and leaving the next day. A very big coincidence. We had dinner and bar-hopped to several places. The thought went through my mind that I wouldn't be able to drink again for a while. . . not that I should. I was honest with my epileptologist that I wouldn't drink unless I had an aura. Or I'd just take an Ativan. For anyone who reads this, do not risk drinking. Do not do what I did. Speaking for myself, I just like to live in the moment when I'm having a good time.

It was comforting to see a familiar face on my quick trip out there. Drinking at the bar past midnight was not the best idea. I got back to my hotel dizzy and dehydrated. I woke up hungover on only three hours of sleep. I could barely pack my bags to head to the airport after the EEG.

On my way out of the hotel, I threw up one last time. The night before could have possibly screwed up the EEG. The more I think about that night, it was worth it, because it was Anthony. I see myself in debt to his generosity. If it wasn't for him, I wouldn't even be here having this surgery. He kept me alive and hopeful, and he saved my life from suicide, the thought of which was constantly racing through my head.

After they put endless electrodes on my head, which took a half-hour, it was finally time to do the test. My head was spinning from the hangover. Attempting to nap for the first hour was a lost cause. I had to NOT throw up on the entire floor.

After a while, it was time to check the baseline of my speech and recall images that the technicians forced in front of my face. The technicians had me associate verbs to the photos with a three-second time limit. It was going so fast for me. With the cognitive decline and hangover, it was even harder. It quickly started.

A sparrow. "Fly." A train. "Ride."

A bunch of pigeons. "Fly." Oops, already used that. Three seconds.

A person praying. "Faith." Is that a verb or a noun?

My brain was working too hard. The next part was testing my right hand. I didn't do this last time. This had me concerned. Was the tumor close to the part that controls my hand function? My right hand was already weakened from my last surgery, and I knew that risk going in. I was right-hand dominant.

I couldn't even throw a baseball. There's a reason for the pitchback in my backyard. All those years of throwing a baseball with my dad are now wasted. Those pre-game tailgates with a football were over. Beer pong? Forget it. Skipping rocks? They went straight into the water. I was fine with a weak hand. I only played golf anyway. My left hand could hold onto the club. Bad golfers always have an excuse, and I used this as mine.

"I'll be back here in a week!" As if the technicians cared.

I'm just glad I got through the EEG without vomiting all over the room. I stumbled back to the Uber. Finally, I flew home. It was cheaper than getting a hotel. And I knew this was going to be the last time I'd be in my house for a while. I couldn't wait to get back to my bed, if only for a short period of time.

## ABBY

The next week came much too quickly. I found myself already booking a one-way ticket because I had no idea when I was coming back after the surgery.

The previous craniotomy lasted a long time, so I didn't know what to expect this time around. Anything can happen. Stepping off the plane was an accomplishment that I committed having them do this again. And this time it was an elective surgery. The doctors discussed the option with me, laying out the risks and benefits. But I was the one who chose to go through with it. From the initial surgery, that damn forty percent, the seizures, and so on. . . I was the one in control. I was in charge of the outcome, whether it was good or bad.

The neurosurgeon said I was only supposed to be in the hospital for five days, max. That was reassuring to me. But that was similar to the last time. The neurosurgeon that would be performing my craniotomy this time was well-established. Journal articles, talks at medical congresses, congress posters, guests on podcasts, and steering committees. I was feeling lucky that I had a neurosurgeon I trusted. I also read a lot about who would be my nurse practitioner. I felt at ease. The plan was set—return home on fewer seizure medications.

I checked into my hotel only to check out less than thirty-six hours before my surgery. I took a PCR COVID-19 test that was mandated by the hospital for all surgeries. I passed. Thank you, Lord. That was a major stress out of the way to have the surgery. If I had COVID-19, I would've been told to quarantine at a hotel.

I'm always one of the few people that still masks up when going through an airport. I can't afford to get COVID-19 for my health. I had more anxiety about testing positive than I had about the surgery.

I was on my way to meet the neurosurgeon for the first time in person. He seemed like a nice enough guy. I also spoke to the nurse, who I had met virtually several weeks earlier.

The first thing I said to the neurosurgeon was, "Err on the side of caution. Do not be aggressive."

"Oh, it's good to know that" he responded.

"Do not make the same mistake as last time," I said, hoping he wouldn't screw up my already dysfunctional brain.

Since this was elective surgery, not necessarily needed at this moment, I was apprehensive about their medical team making a mistake and ruining my quality of life some more. Please give me hope for once. Make my life better in some way. I went back to my hotel and actually slept until my early wake-up call came around.

Surprisingly, I showed up at the hospital without a care in the world. I made sure to remember the Kanye West song this time, *All of the Lights*. I listened to it over and over. I made my way to the surgery waiting room. I was pumped up while all the others waited impatiently for their surgeries. I could see that they were nervous, and I caught a few sweating. Meanwhile, I was still vibing hard to Kanye and almost missed my name being called.

Disclaimer: This was before everyone knew Kanye was antisemitic.

"Power off your cell phone," the woman at the front desk told me.

I signed some release forms before getting undressed and hopping on the stretcher. My feet didn't hit the floor. I was smiling. I was excited. I was alone, in a different area of the country, and still I wasn't nervous. It was a complete 180° from the original surgery.

The nurse came in.

"Hi Joseph, my name is Abigail."

"Oh, what's up?" My tone gave off such an over-confident response for someone who's about to get a drill to his skull in fifteen minutes.

"You can call me Abby."

"My first dog was named Abby! She was a dachshund."

"Oh really! It's a great name. It's unique."

Suddenly, my bed was being passed along to the anesthesiologist. He was asking me a bunch of questions, not knowing that I wasn't nervous at all. He knew I was a pharmacist and asked what therapeutic area I specialized in. I was providing him with a little education on what I had been working on. At the same time, this anesthesiologist mentioned an article that was relevant to the Epstein Barr-Virus. Some nerdy small talk. He wouldn't stop though.

As soon as he did, I asked, "Can we do the countdown?" He said, "Sure, start!"

"Ten. . ."

I awoke to someone waving in my face. "Dachshund!" I shouted.

She cracked up. The doctor was so confused. He must've thought I was freaking out.

"We have an inside joke!" she exclaimed.

The doctor had more important things to do. But it was all the same tasks as last time. It was all "Repeat this line" or "What does this picture show?" Then we had a natural conversation as the neurosurgeon was operating. He needed a constant flow of words, waiting until my speech started to decline. When my speech started to go out, he would remove his instruments. This was all expected.

I thought I would be a little scared. But I wasn't. I was awake and aware, as if I was laying on the couch watching a movie; fully conscious of everything around me. I was trying to hold still and thinking I wouldn't have to go through this surgery again. It was all going well. It seemed too good for my luck. All the tasks ended.

The doctor was playing around back there. Abby watched me for a while. I didn't know what was going on.

My right hand and leg jumped from the table. "There it goes!" she yelled.

He tried again. The same thing happened.

I felt like a puppet being controlled by a string. I wanted to tell him to stop. Maybe he'll get the point of not poking that area again. He kept trying to mess around with that area and eventually, he stopped.

I was awake for probably an hour. And there were major milestones that were hit. There were no seizures, and he completed the surgery on time. That's how every brain surgery should be done.

I woke up to a "Good job, Joe. Excellent job!"

The first thought I had was, I didn't do anything except lie flat. My neurosurgeon and his staff had just completed a hundred or two-thousand-dollar surgery. Health insurance is a savior.

I didn't say anything on purpose, even though I had the ability to. I didn't want to jinx it in case anything went wrong. I just rested. Then, off to the PACU I went.


## HANDS

The first couple of days were confusing for me. I couldn't tell left from right. I couldn't answer simple questions like "Where are we?" I couldn't read or comprehend anything. I couldn't organize my thoughts. I was alive but in an abyss that was completely void of any thing but movement.

A nurse called my dad every day to give him my recovery status. Dad trickled that information down to a group of trusted friends—who were told to keep it hush from others that may have found out. I told very few people, as I did in the past. Unfortunately, I had no visitors with me because of the distance. Others pleaded to visit me though. I rejected the offer—a selfish thing for me to do that made me a hypocrite of my own words: "Do it for them."

I told my dad to stay home to watch my dog. There was no sense flying out to be with me. I was only sitting in a hospital bedroom and renting out a hotel after.

I only let my dad come for a week for two specific reasons. Number one: hospitals require someone who is staying inpatient to be released by a friend or family member. Number two: the British Open was on TV and I wanted to watch it with him.

I was lying in the hotel room when I heard a buzz. It was a text from my manager. "When are you coming back to work?" I wanted to tell him to fuck off. I didn't say that. I'm on medical leave. It's a good thing I couldn't spell or piece together a text back as a response.

As soon as my dad left, I stayed at the hotel because my brain issues of understanding hadn't resolved yet. This probably wasn't the best idea. I didn't realize how much I actually needed him there. I was confused. Standing at an intersection, not knowing what green and red stood for, and confused about when it was time to walk. . . I walked right into traffic. God had all the cars swerve around me like Moses parting the Red Sea. But I survived. No harm, no foul.

I just had to make it past this big city and get home to my bed.

As soon as I got back to the hotel from eating lunch, I received a call from a friend, Lindsay. It was a pleasant conversation. My speech was illegible, same as the previous surgery, so Lindsay understood. We spoke about my healing plan, and I was upset that I would miss her wedding. She asked if I had any seizures since the surgery a week ago.

"Nope!"

At that point, I hadn't spoken to any of my friends except through my dad's text messages. As soon as I hung up, I could feel something was wrong. I didn't know what, but I was very concerned about what was happening to my body. I reached for one of my medications. I slowly watched the bottle fall, and pills crawled all over the floor. I wiped my limp hand across the drugs. I could see the pills move, but I couldn't feel them. My right hand went numb.

I wasn't sure if any feeling in the right hand would come back. I shook my arm, but I couldn't feel anything from the wrist down. I used my left hand and took all my seizure medications at once. It was a tense moment I'll never forget—just waiting and waiting to see what would happen. At that moment, I could slowly open and close my right hand, but no feeling in the fingers yet. It took thirty minutes until all the feeling in my right hand came back.

A hand seizure? *So, I must deal with my regular mouth-twitching seizures, and now this hand seizure thing?*

This was not the plan! I was supposed to have a reduction of lip-twitching seizures, but now I've added another kind. I had a sense something else would go wrong. It was too convenient for something ever to work out how it was supposed to. *Fulton luck.* Having craniotomies just wasn't my thing. I'd have to return to my favorite place. . .

Having been to the hospital so many times, I knew how to skip the line in the ER waiting room. I had waited in the ER too many times in the past only to realize I'd just sit there for several hours. I paid my dues enough times. For once I had to use the "my heart hurts" trick. It didn't seem like anyone in the ER was having a heart attack at the moment.

"Hello, my name is Joe Fulton. My whole right hand went numb and I don't know what it was. Also, my heart keeps fluttering."

"Okay, have a seat, Mr. Fulton." Two seconds later.

"Mr. Fulton. I'll take you back for processing."

I sat down with this nurse. Having to explain what happened frightened me. My right hand was shaking. I had to check if my left hand was shaking as well, just to prove it wasn't nervousness. I don't know the medical terminology for what I was experiencing.

"My right hand just went numb. I had a craniotomy to reduce seizures. Maybe this has something to do with it." I remained calm. Freaking out would do no good.

I struggled with the words in that sentence. I struggled with the details. I was hoping someone would figure this out for me. But nope. As soon as I was processed, someone pulled me out of the door, stripped me down to nearly nothing, and threw a robe at me.

It was a woman in a flowery scrub cap. "Wear these socks and put this gown on," she said.

This was a repeat of my ongoing hell. I wanted at least one break from all these hospital visits. Not here, not now. I knew this gown situation meant that I was going to be admitted. I just wanted to be released, but with a condition like this, I deserved to be put back in the hospital no matter how much it sucked.

Slowly, I was coming to terms with the fact that this surgery may have been a mistake. I was in for a long night to try to understand what was happening—an EKG, CT scan, MRI, and so on.

After all these tests, the woman wearing the flowery scrub cap was standing over me. Her phone rang. It was from a radiologist in the hospital. They were giving her a status update on a patient.

Unfortunately for the patient, it was not good news. That's when I figured out that I was the patient. And the "not good news" was for me. I listened as best as I could.

"Infarct."

I knew the term. I asked her if it was true what I heard. All I could get out of her was a light nod and tears as soon as I grabbed her hand. I was holding back tears myself. She must've been fifteen years older than me. She was looking down at a man in the prime of his life. Going through this surgery cost me everything I worked hard for.

"I'll go grab some tissues," she said. She meant it for her and me. Once she got back, the doctor clasped her hand with mine. She had a great bedside manner, an emotional bedside manner. It was a busy night in the hospital, but she returned to me whenever she could. I still had many more tests to go.

Twelve hours later, I was finally in a room with a man strapping electrodes to my head to monitor for seizure activity. I had so many people hovering around me. The crew of doctors, nurses, and pharmacists were putting their bright minds together to explain what happened. At that point, I was convinced that the neurosurgeon did some damage—damage that made me regret the thought of coming all the way out here. But it was my decision.

What are they saying about me? Is it about the infarct? Something about a possible hemorrhage?

The nurse gave me a steroid, which was a big mistake. I had been awake for nearly twenty-four hours and was going delirious. That steroid made me extremely hungry—so hungry that I was in pain. I hadn't eaten since breakfast the day before. With a freshly operated brain, hunger, and lack of sleep, that was the perfect formula for a seizure. I was writhing in pain and shouting for food. I would've taken a fruit cup or some Jell-O.

Curled up in a ball, I was begging the doctors to feed me.

The technician who was still placing electrodes on my head said, "He's just making it up."

After that comment, I went batshit crazy. I was kicking pillows and blankets and trying to shake the bed. I was in serious pain, and I wanted to kick his ass—except I couldn't because I was restrained by three people.

The good thing about staying in the hospital was having multiple MRIs to eventually rule out the possibility of an infarct in my brain. Plus, I had additional rehabilitation, including more physical therapy, occupational therapy, speech therapy, and doctors all around to monitor my progress.

This time I could leave the bed or couch without the alarm sounding. And I did have some entertainment. A certain occupational therapist used to check on me several times a day. Every day, I'd have to make sure my smock was clean and that I didn't have any food in my beard. It was clear I didn't need her services, and she was wasting her time spending it on me. All she did was come in to hang out. But through that, we formed a brief crush.

All the rest was Murphy's Law. My primary neurosurgeon caught COVID-19, and the nurse practitioner went on vacation. They were the ones in charge and the only people that could set me free. Spending the final days there felt nauseating. And my insurance bills were mounting quickly. All I could imagine was how much fun my nurse practitioner was having. Instead, my vacation was this. . . spent here. . . in a hospital.

I have some good friends in the area, which I am thankful for. The one who released me is a physician out there—a big up-and-coming doctor and the number one fan of "The Bachelor." He and his wife were living a short walk from my hotel. I can't thank them enough for being who they are and living where they live, but mostly, helping me out and making me feel confident. Listening to my muffled and slow voice without judgment felt nice. My sanity was briefly restored.

I finally left that city, twenty-six days later. My speech hadn't come back fully, and speech therapy wasn't helping. All the doctors involved in my care were concerned because I couldn't pronounce my words correctly. Sometimes, not at all.

I'm likely to be in speech therapy for the same duration as last time, which was a little over two years. I am still having both hand and mouth seizures. Every day was like the other.

My manager didn't wish me well at all, rather, constantly checked on when I would be back to work. "We need to talk about your employment at this company," his text read.

## THE LOYAL ONE

The day I arrived home, there was only one buddy I wanted to see: not a human, but my dog, Skip—a joyful eight-year-old Lab-Pit mix who is Lab in the body and Pit in the face. His favorite things to do: sleeping, eating, going on walks, and being everywhere that I am. He's a kind rescue animal who just wants a happy home.

I immediately noticed something right away that didn't seem right. It was a growth sticking out of his back left side. My dad called him a "Diva" while showing me how he's been feeding him, holding food up to his face. He was drooling. He was barely drinking. My dad did not pick up the signs that I observed right away. The day I get home to hopefully recover is the day I must care for another.

I monitored Skip for a day. He wouldn't eat on his own, and he's always ready to munch on something. He was regurgitating when he drank water, which was a serious sign that there was something wrong. The veterinarian told me he was having gastrointestinal issues. I gave him some medication, but he was just not right. He kept regurgitating. I took him back to the veterinarian once I finished giving him the drugs. Skip was still having issues. The veterinarian disregarded his new growth because apparently most dogs have them and they're just made of fat.

But my dog wasn't a typical dog. He was a Fulton dog who had the *Fulton luck.*

Blaming it on gastrointestinal issues was just not right. Skip's never had problems with his gut, and being on all these medications was not helping. It got to the point where he was vomiting and spitting up fluids every day. I was trying to be there for him as much as I could.

There is carpet in every room in my house and rugs in the family room, living room, and dining room. The stink of my house started getting to me. Since Skip wanted to be near me, I decided to stay with him in the kitchen. At all hours of the day, I was recovering there with him. I had red marks and bruises from sleeping on the hard kitchen floor. I prayed his new medication would start working.

"There's something wrong with him!"

"Gastrointestinal issues. I went to veterinarian school. Trust me." This cocky veterinarian was telling me off. If I wasn't having so many brain issues of my own, I could fend for myself. But I really couldn't speak.

I took Skip back to the veterinarian, again, since he wasn't healing like I thought he would. He went almost a week without eating. I was going crazy because I was still trying to heal myself. Fix my dog!

That's when the veterinarian spotted something I hadn't noticed. There wasn't just one growth. These were everywhere. They were enlarged mast cells spanning across his whole body, but unfortunately, I didn't know if I caught it in time.

I yelled as much as I could, "Give him the works. CBC, ultrasound, biopsy, whatever you're paid to do." My words didn't come out clearly, but the veterinarian got the message.

When I heard the word "Tumor," it brought back the bad news of when I first got diagnosed. Apparently, mast cell tumors are quite common in dogs. But why my dog? He's an innocent dog who has done nothing wrong in his life but has cancer. I'm full of sins, but my dog cannot be; he doesn't even bite! I'm fair game for cancer to strike, but not Skip.

Both of us, under one roof, have cancer. I received much more sympathy from friends for Skip than I ever had, and rightfully so—he's perfect.

I was experiencing cancer from the other side now. First, I had cancer, but I understood nobody else could do anything. Now he has cancer, and there's nothing I can do. There was only one of two conclusions I could come up with: God's testing how well I can take care of others, OR Skip's trying to play the cancer card and steal my thunder. We're now cancer buddies.

I felt like a bad owner. But I did what I needed to do. Surgery, two infections, constant medications, dozens of veterinarian appointments, a lack of sleep for two months, and a total cost of over $15,000. Dealing with all of this was not only stressful, but it also impacted my ability to recover.

But what's the other option? Let Skip die? He is always there for me. Even if I had racked up hospital bills that I'll never pay off, I needed Skip more.

He was left with an awesome scar.

# CHAPTER 8:

# A BEAUTIFUL LIFE

"Your eyes don't match your smile." That was what I told this woman when I first met her. I could tell something was hidden behind those green eyes. And without a doubt, there was.

We shared stories about our wounds. Wept a little. A lot. That instant connection turned us quickly into friends. I asked her to share a bit about her mother's diagnosis of breast cancer for this book. These are her words:

Our story starts twenty years ago this month on Labor Day weekend, 1998. Titanic was in theaters that year. My mom was thirty-eight years old. I was seven, and my little sister, Anna, was four. My mom was an elementary school teacher in our small town. She loved her job. She and my dad were avid water skiers. Her parents—my grandparents—had recently retired and moved back home from down south and now lived just a few miles away from us. Life was good.

On this particular September day, I remember the entire family milling around in our front yard in a confused panic. My mom was on the phone. She was getting the news that she had an extremely aggressive form of breast cancer. It was not caught early by any means. She had four large tumors, and the cancer had spread to her lymph nodes, having been allowed to grow unchecked after an entire year of misdiagnosis. She had gone to her doctor four times and been refused a mammogram each time but the last.

We all cried. I think Anna probably just cried because we were crying because she really didn't know what was happening. My mom said she was terrified thinking about Anna. She was so little that she didn't even know how to tie her shoes yet. She prayed, "God, please just let me raise my girls."

A few weeks later, my mom started a tough chemotherapy regimen under the care of a top oncologist in the city about an hour away. In the parking lot of my elementary school, I remember clumps of her hair falling out and floating away with the wind. When we got home that day, she let me cut all of her hair off. My sister played with a Barbie doll in the background and promptly nicknamed my mom "Baldie." She was our comic relief.

Over the next few months, Mom let me help her with a lot of things. She let me help her with getting the injections ready, draining her surgical drains after her bilateral mastectomy, and even going to appointments with various doctors. Even though I was just seven, she let me be a part of the team.

I would sit on the bathroom floor when she took a bubble bath to unwind after a tough day, and we would just talk. It was during the bubble baths that I learned you can simultaneously be incredibly tough but show emotion and cry at the same time. She showed me what real bravery looks like—she embodied it.

When I cried about her being sick, my mom would talk me through it time and time again. At the end of the conversation, she always told me to put it in perspective. She'd say things about how she had good doctors now and how we were still having fun no matter what. I didn't know that there were conversations about taping videos for Anna and me in case she died. She was not expected to live, but incredibly, she did. The chemotherapy, surgery, and radiation worked. Her hair grew back into a cute little pixie cut, and life was good.

In January 2000, Mom found a few bumps under her skin near her surgical scar. On an ice-cold winter's night, I ran across the snow-covered yard from playing at the neighbor's house to find out that the cancer had returned.

My mom took the second diagnosis in stride. It was a local recurrence, which meant it was just in her skin and not in any critical organs. On the other hand, I was beyond crushed. When you're nine, you haven't really grasped the nuances of local recurrences yet. You just hear the words cancer. . . and again. . . and you lose it. I was at an age where people's grandparents weren't even sick yet, and I couldn't bear the thought of my mom going through the hell that is cancer one more time. My mom's spirits were high, she was confident, and she lifted me up alongside her and showed me how to be resilient in the face of a setback.

Her chemotherapy this time was a targeted drug, meaning that she didn't have to lose her hair, so she flew under the radar as a cancer patient a lot more in her day-to-day life. This made things a little easier in public. In addition, since this round of cancer required less aggressive chemotherapy than the last, she was able to have her infusions with all these older men at the cancer center in our town.

Mom did not have to drive down to the big cancer center in the city like she had the first time. She loved to make all of them laugh, bringing some joy to the local grandpas getting prostate or skin cancer treatment. She could really elevate everyone's mood in the room, no matter what situation the people in the room were in.

My mom took off from work during the year of her second diagnosis because her immune system was being compromised and her back-to-back cancer-related appointments made it impossible for her job. Since she wasn't working, this meant she could drive me to fourth grade every day.

She would hop in the car right after getting a shower with her pixie-cut hair all crazy.

Every morning, she looked at me from the driver's seat with the utmost seriousness. She would ask, "Kramer or the Unabomber?" She wanted to know if I wanted her to let everyone see her crazy hair like Kramer from "Seinfeld" when she dropped me off at school, or did I want her to put up the hood of her hoodie to cover the crazy hair but look like the infamous sketch of the Unabomber? I picked the Unabomber every single day, and we had so much fun. My mom, aka the Unabomber, was good at putting things in perspective.

Through her experiences, she was a support for so many people that were diagnosed with cancer too, especially other young people. She never wanted to be the poster child for cancer; she didn't want any special attention. She just wanted to help people. Women she didn't even know would be given our home phone number, newly diagnosed with breast cancer, and my mom would spend hours on the phone encouraging them, crying with them, and making them laugh. They would call without any prior notice, and my mom would drop everything to just sit on the phone and talk with them.

Sometimes I would sit next to her in our living room with my head on her lap and just listen to her. She made lifelong friends on those phone calls, some of whom she never even met in person. It was really hard on her when the lives of many of those women were cut short by cancer. It was another reminder to put life in perspective because it is not guaranteed.

Years passed. I was home from university in the city after finishing my sophomore year. My sister was about to start her senior year of high school. My mom was now the director of special education at a local school district, advocating for kids with disabilities and still loving her job. She was still waterskiing with my dad, and all of us were still having dinner at home with my grandparents most weeknights.

It was a sunny day in July when we found out that after over a decade, the cancer had come back a third time. This time it had metastasized to her lungs. For those of you who aren't familiar, this means that the original cancer had traveled and found a new place to grow in my mom's lungs. It's situations like this that make cancer of non-essential body parts like breasts really dangerous, even fatal. She had so much trouble with breathing and was rail thin because she couldn't keep down food while coughing non-stop. This time, I was older, halfway through an undergraduate degree in the sciences, and I understood way more about her situation. I was scared out of my mind.

I didn't want to go back to school that semester—I wanted to take a semester off to help my mom. But my mom encouraged me to continue my education as planned. So I did. For this round of chemotherapy, she got her infusions at the same place as thirteen years ago at the big medical center in the city. The center was about six blocks from my college apartment, so I would walk down and sit with her during treatment.

They had free snacks for the patients and their families, which was great because free food is, of course, a coveted prize for a college student. More importantly, I got to just hang out with my best friend. Mom was friends with everyone in the place, since she had been a patient at that clinic for thirteen years. The only people she didn't know were the newest patients, and even that didn't last long. If she spotted someone new in the infusion chair across from her, she would lean over and gently ask, "Is this your first treatment?"

With tears in their eyes, they would quietly say that it was. Moreover, from her own chair, hooked up to machines herself, with a beautiful smile and the kindest heart, she would chat with them and give them a little pep talk to help them through their first day in this horrible and unfamiliar world that she was so experienced in. I just sat by and smiled, sad and proud and grateful all at the same time. She was unstoppable.

Against all odds, she recovered one more time. She saw me graduate college and start my first job in clinical trials at the local cancer center. It was a tough job. I saw the chaos behind the scenes of taking care of complicated cancer cases, where mistakes can cost patients their lives. Mom helped me with the emotional toll of this job through our daily phone calls, giving me the incredible support only she could provide. She continued with treatment, as she would have to be on some form of chemotherapy for the rest of her life to keep metastatic cancer at bay. But life was still good.

A year after college, I quit my job at the cancer center to pursue a research doctorate. It was my dream, but it led me to move several states away from my family. I loved my lab, new friends, and my program, but I hated being away from my mom. The program was five years long, so I had to buckle down for a long separation.

Our phone calls increased to several times a day due to the major stresses of a PhD program and how much I missed her. On those calls, she kept me updated on all that was going on at home. She had minor setbacks from different treatments. These setbacks were weird ones, like it affecting her skin such that her fingerprints rubbed away, or mouth sores that led to severe dehydration and an overnight stay at the hospital.

As always, she handled things in stride. However, even a year or so into my program, I never adjusted to the distance. I always worried about her and missed her terribly. Admittedly, my separation anxiety was probably partially caused by her illness in my formative years.

One particular phone conversation stands out. I was in the middle of my second year of graduate school. It was during the holidays. I sat in my apartment and sobbed to her on the phone about being apart. She told me gently that it would be okay, that I was pursuing a dream of mine, and that it was just temporary. We would be together again when school was over.

Just three months after that conversation, my mom was diagnosed with an extremely aggressive form of leukemia.

I was in my statistics class when I stepped outside to take her call about the diagnosis. I ran sobbing to my lab across the south quadrant to gather my things and then go home to my apartment and pack. The next morning at 6:00 a.m., my boyfriend dropped me off at the airport to fly home.

All of the chemotherapy my mom had over the years for the treatment of her breast cancer had caused a second completely different cancer, a worse diagnosis than any of the previous times. It was rare, but it was happening. To her. Again. If you're counting, this was diagnosis number four. She was just fifty-six years old.

When I got there, the prognosis was so bad that a few doctors suggested that we just go home and live out the rest of her days. My best estimate is that she probably would have had about three weeks to live without treatment, if not less. This cancer was aggressive. I told her I would support her no matter what she chose. I was twenty-four, Anna was twenty-one; we were young, but we were grown. She had done everything she could to raise us despite the circumstances, which was all she wanted to do those many years ago when she received her first cancer diagnosis. I told her I would love her just as much if she decided not to pursue treatment.

She told me, "I had a good life. I'm doing this for you and Anna." She was nothing if not stubborn.

This treatment was inpatient—she would be in the hospital for at least a month, if not much longer. It was at the hospital I'd worked at just a few years before. She was on a really rough cocktail of chemotherapy for a week straight, twenty-four hours a day. Things got so bad that my dad, my sister, and I took turns sleeping in a chair in her room every single night to make sure she wouldn't die of flash pulmonary edema, which almost happened several different times. I would lie in the chair and just listen to her breathe to make sure she still could.

There were mistakes like crazy, despite the kindness of many of the doctors and nurses. Since her previous oncologist was a breast cancer specialist and was in a different hospital across town, we couldn't have him on the case. We didn't have her usual care team. People were dropping the ball. Her kidneys and lungs failed, and she went on and off a ventilator and dialysis. As always, she was graceful and kind and loving, even though she was in so much pain.

On the other hand, I was not in the mood to feel kind. I was infuriated. I watched all the different teams, hematology, oncology, pulmonology, nephrology, and internal medicine. All made what seemed like very avoidable mistakes. Infectious disease was the only team that seemed on top of it because the attending physician was consistent and not rotating on and off service.

The teams didn't communicate with each other. They just let my mom circle the drain because this case was too complicated, even though it was supposed to be a Top 10 hospital in the country. I watched people continue to screw up, and my mom would pay for it, ending up back in the ICU from the main treatment floor with even more complications than before. The chemotherapy was working, although it was almost killing her with side effects. If I could just keep her alive, she might have a shot for a bone marrow transplant and a recovery.

I called a meeting with eight attending physicians to discuss her case. My hands were shaking as I watched them all walk in with their coffee. I was twenty-four, just a young and inexperienced student, but nevertheless, I had watched the person I love the most struggle with cancer for seventeen years. At that moment, I was at my breaking point. Once they all sat down at the long conference table, I politely chewed out some of the top physicians in the country.

I said, quivering, "I know she's a complicated case. I've worked here, so I've seen what happens. But she's my mother. So, you all need to work together to do what you can."

I vividly remember my mom's face from across the ICU as I watched my dad tell her what I said in the meeting. As sick as she was, I know she still found some comfort just knowing that I was watching out for her. I would have done anything to keep her safe. I was probably the most aggressive family member of a patient that these people had ever seen. I knew deep down they all hated me, but I didn't care. Incredibly, things started to improve, and teams began to communicate better. I think they were genuinely slightly scared of me.

Because of the care team's diligence and Mom's incredible strength, she began to stabilize. We enjoyed ourselves, even in the hospital. Mom texted Anna and me after a few days of telling stories, take-out food, and quietly listening to our favorite songs in the ICU. She said, "Thanks for the memories, girls. The last few days have been fabulous."

She learned how to walk again in rehab. Her bone marrow biopsy showed no more leukemia. And on a beautiful spring day on my twenty-fifth birthday, after waking up in a chair in my mom's room at the rehab facility, I got the best present I will ever get. I got to take her home. She told me, "This feels like the end of the movie." It really did.

After a few weeks at home, Mom was doing so well, I got the opportunity to go back to grad school after a months-long leave of absence. I walked into the office, and my boss ran and hugged me like I had won a Nobel Prize. I started excitedly doing experiments. I went back to calling my mom every day, which was our treasured routine. I was planning my next visit home to see her. Life was good.

A few weeks later, I was sitting in my lab on a Friday afternoon, preparing for a weekend experiment, when I got one final devastating call. Out of what seemed like nowhere, things had gone downhill in a matter of hours. I drove five hundred miles through five different states, leaving voicemails on her phone that I knew she would never hear as I drove and drove and drove. I ran into the hospital at full speed.

Within the hour, I held my mom's hand when she died. The last few minutes, she didn't really know what was going on, but I knew that she trusted me. I told her she was going to get out of the hospital. She smiled at me one last time, and then she was gone.

The past two and a half years have been extremely difficult. Life has not been that good. We had a huge party to celebrate her life instead of a funeral, which is exactly what she would have wanted. I'm so happy that she doesn't have to hurt anymore, but I'm completely devastated to be without her. Some people were surprised that I came back to school—but PhD students are notoriously depressed, so I said if I'm going to be grieving and miserable, I might as well get a PhD out of it. That's my best attempt at a joke.

Next month I'm defending my dissertation and moving across the country again. I still reach for the phone to call her. A part of life feels like if I can't share it with her, it doesn't feel like it's even really happening. My mom was the light of my life, and she still is. I know how insanely lucky I was to have her for twenty-five years. And I'm going to squeeze as much out of life as possible because that's what she fought for.

Things are not easy without my mentor and my very best friend. But, whenever I'd be struggling with something in my life, I'd say, "I can do it," to encourage myself, and my mom would reply, "You ARE doing it!" She would be reminding me that it just takes a little change in perspective to see that you're actively making it through whatever difficulty you're having at that moment. I hope her memory brings a little strength to whatever situation you're going through right now. Whatever it is, you're doing it!

# EPILOGUE

*Writing is a way to etch messages into eternity.*

I wrote a single paragraph of this book four years ago and then stopped. It just wasn't the right time. In the months after my second brain surgery, I heard from Maddie. She's now married with a baby, and I could not be happier for her. To my surprise, she said, "How's your book going?" Maddie knew I would express raw emotions and be ready for the words used against her. She didn't care about that. "You have a story worth telling."

And that was the catalyst I needed. So, I buckled down and wrote this book months after brain surgery. To say my mental state and Skip's battle with cancer didn't affect the writing of this book would be a lie. Please excuse any errors in this book and the things I don't recall well. But I'm delighted to get my battle with cancer down on paper.

Reliving this story wasn't an easy feat to get through. And as we speak, I'm still dealing with the main topics of this book all over again. But I think cancer really gave me a different view on life. I feel lucky I was given the chance to face adversity, and I am thankful for everything I've overcome. That's something no one can take away.

Thank you to all those for allowing me to share this with their personal stories. I will never do justice to all the departed souls listed in this book. To the ones that continue to fight—fight away. You inspire others.

Thank you to all the doctors, nurses, and medical staff who will remain anonymous for privacy reasons. To my friends, family, and extended family, I couldn't be as positive and hopeful without your love.

I'd love to hear your own stories; they deserve to be shared.